THE ADDICT'S LOOP

A New Understanding And Workbook For

Codependent Relationships

And Addiction

By Rene Eram

Contents:

Chapter 12: Glossary. Page 143

At the end of the book there are a few pages for your notes. More essays on codependence and addiction can be read on my website, **www.theaddictsloop.com.**

Introduction

This book may change the way you see the world and your surrounding relationships. It will give you new terms to learn as it breaks down the destructive and unconscious jigsaw pieces of codependence and addiction. It will uncover powerful unconscious codependent and addiction patterns that are inherited and learned during childhood years. In the beginning you will read how codependence and addiction are inherited, programmed and passed down through generations and families. It will take you into scenarios and examples to learn how the various components and deeper mechanics of codependence and addiction unconsciously manipulate and control your behavior and life. You will learn how codependence and addiction originated and evolved and its deeper characteristics and behavior. You will learn about the addict's loop and how to identify it in your life. You will also learn about the biochemical loop and how both loops evolved and mimic each other.

This book will show you how to examine your love relationships and disentangle yourself from the deep unconscious patterns of codependence. You will learn how addicts change and react differently in codependence. It will take you through various questions and answers and into a workbook with a nine step counter-conditioning process. I am hopeful this book will help you understand how you got here, what codependence and addiction really are and how to go forth and live a truly authentic life, rich with love.

During several of my workshops, I discovered patterns that create a destructive loop in the addict's unconscious. With this new understanding of inherited codependence and addiction patterns, I set out to answer several questions:

What creates addiction?
Why do some people become addicts and others don't?
Why do some addicts become full blown in their teen years and others later in life?

Why are addicts in denial about their addiction?
Why do some addicts come from loving homes where no addiction,
abuse or trauma occurred?
Does an addict love his addiction more than his loved ones?
What can families do to help an addict they love?
Why does addiction progress and lead to insanity and sometimes
death?
What causes the Dr. Jekyll and Mr. Hyde personalities of
addiction?
What is the cure or strongest treatment for recovery?

This book will give you concise answers and a deeper
understanding of all the questions above.

There is a difference between unconscious and subconscious.
These are words which are used a number of times. Unconscious
means below your conscious radar and is completely unknown.
The unconscious world can be repressed abuse, trauma, feelings,
fears, thought patterns or obsessions that are completely blocked
and hidden from consciousness. *Subconscious* exists right below
consciousness. An example of subconscious could be your street
address; you may not be thinking of it right now, but if asked, you
could pull it up from your subconscious.

In this book I do not separate alcoholism from addiction. All
addictive patterns are included when I use the word "addiction" or
"fixes."

There is new terminology to describe the codependence and
addiction model. You can find all terminology in the Glossary.
This book may become confusing if not read in order. It is part
educational and part workbook, with writing exercises and self-
actualization tools to help create healthy boundaries and counter
condition unconscious codependence and addiction patterns. The
goal of this book is to make the complicated patterns of
codependence and addiction understandable and create new and
effective tools for your recovery. In the future I will have tutorial
videos on my website, www.theaddictsloop.com, to help guide you
and explain some of the concepts in the book. Consider this a

starter kit to counter-condition unconscious addiction and codependence patterns. More importantly, *"What do you identify with and what resonates in you?"* I encourage you to write in the book, underline, highlight, re-read and talk about what you learn. This is where your journey begins ...

Chapter 1

Codependence

Codependence – Codependence is defined as a psychological condition or a relationship in which a person is unconsciously controlled or manipulated by another who is affected with a pathological condition (addiction or illness). In broader terms, it refers to the unconscious dependence on the needs of or control of another.

The two codependent roles I focus on are the "controller" and the "dependent." Both codependent roles are inherited, unconscious and learned during child and teen years.

Controller - The *controller* child is programmed and learns to be controlling and enabling and rescues people who have inherited the *dependent* role. *Remember, most of the controller's behavior is unconscious (no awareness).* Listed below are some of the typical characteristics and behavior of the controller.

1) Controller can be extremely aggressive, arrogant and feel "better than."

2) Controller will offer advice whether asked for or not.

3) Controller can get depressed and feel "less than" but tends to rise out of his low self esteem and emotional pain to "run the show," be the leader and in control.

4) Controller can be bossy, dominating and critical toward the dependent and others.

5) Controller will ignore his own needs and become obsessive about rescuing and enabling the dependent.

6) Controller will take on too much of the relationship responsibility, feel used and not appreciated and become a victim

of the dependent.

7) If the controller feels he is losing control of a situation, his micro managing and controlling behavior can get worse.

8) Controller often doesn't trust the dependent to do anything right.

9) Controller will believe his way is the best and be highly critical of the dependent or another person's advice.

Many of the controller's characteristics and behavior can be dormant until the controller enters into an intimate relationship with a dependent.

Dependent - The *dependent* child is programmed and learns to be broken, shameful, needy, and "less than" and feels entitled to be rescued and saved by the controller. *Remember, most of the dependent's behavior is unconscious (no awareness).* Some of the characteristics of the dependent are listed below.

1) Dependent dishonestly "people pleases" to feel accepted and loved by his controller(s). *"People pleasing" is saying "yes" when you mean "no" and agreeing to things when you don't agree.*

2) Dependent is programmed to feel "less than" and broken. Instead of rising out of his pain like the controller, the dependent believes he deserves the pain and will repress and carry it.

3) Dependent will perform and be the "nice person" everyone likes.

5) Because the dependent "people pleases" and learns to believe his own voice and root honesty don't count, he becomes detached from his feelings and has difficulties knowing what he *feels*.

6) Dependent does not like confrontation and becomes passive aggressive and manipulates from a doormat position.

The following are examples of passive-aggressive behavior.

Controller asks his dependent partner to leave some orange juice for him in the morning. The dependent partner drinks the last bit of OJ every time. A female controller asks her dependent partner to leave the toilet seat down and her male dependent partner leaves it up. The female or male controller is on a diet and asks the dependent not to buy any ice cream, the dependent shows up with a pint of their favorite kind. A controller will ask the dependent partner not to fix something (plumbing, electrical, etc.) and the dependent partner will attempt to fix it and break it. The controller tells the dependent partner what she really likes sexually but the dependent partner will continually not do it. The controller asks the dependent to recycle bottles and cans but the controller keeps finding them in the garbage can. Dependent could be considered a covert and subtle tyrant.

7) Dependent can seem lazy, irresponsible and spoiled and leans on the controller to carry and run his life.

8) Dependent will gain momentum and show signs of being responsible and then sabotage his success and return to being defeated, needy and "less than."

9) When controller is critical of the dependent, the dependent will sometimes withdraw, become a victim and hold back affection.

10) The dependent believes he is a victim of the world's wrong doings and blames others for making him broken and weak.

Many of the dependent's characteristics and behavior can be dormant until the dependent enters into an intimate relationship with a controller.

The inherited codependent roles of the *controller* and *dependent* are determined before birth, carry destructive programming that becomes the child's learned behavior and continue throughout the codependent's life. The child survives his codependent family and significant role models by unconsciously adapting and taking on the destructive codependent role(s), which forces him to abandon his authentic self and root honesty.

The Unconscious Codependent Roles Of The Controller and Dependent.

The Controller

The controller child ("child" includes teen years) grows up feeling insecure and disconnected from his family and role models. The controller child spends hours alone, thinking *"if only I were smarter, taller, better looking or perfect they would love me."* The child begins personalizing the family conflicts and feels responsible for solving the family problems. To survive, the child unconsciously splits from his authentic self to become a controlling pretend-parent toward the family dependent(s). The codependent split from his authentic self creates obsessive compulsive thinking and behavior.

Being the controller gives the child the experience of feeling loved, powerful and needed. The child's efforts create the illusion of being a hero who must constantly rescue and enable the family dependent(s). The dependent role is programmed to be "temporarily saved" but then returns to being needy and broken, which makes the controller child feel like a failure and abandoned. The controller's obsession to save the entitled and broken dependent creates a destructive definition of love; *"I am loved, honored and praised because you need me to rescue and enable you."* The controller's definition of love is soon followed by rejection and abandonment. This becomes the revolving-door pattern of the child controller.

An example of the *controller* role is a male child-controller and his *dependent* father. It could also be a daughter/mother or daughter/father or any combination, but for this example it is father/son. The father is unemployed and feels broken and needy and leans on his controller son for emotional support. The controller son talks to his father and tries to make him happy and confident. He tells his father that he believes in him and promises his dad *"everything will be okay."* Later that day, the father feels better and puts on his suit. The father hugs and thanks his son and says, *"I don't know what I'd do without you."* The father then leaves and looks for a job. The controller son feels in control and a euphoric high for "fixing" his father's depression and sadness. Later that night, his dependent father lies on the couch, sad and depressed, and tells his son, *"What's the point of putting on a suit, I'll never find a job."* The controller son's euphoric bubble bursts and the young son now feels fear and anxiety and once again attempts to rescue his dependent father. *Because both roles are unconscious (no awareness), the dependent father may not realize he's leaning on and baiting his son to rescue him. The controller child can only focus on rescuing his dependent father and recreating their euphoric "high" connection so the controller child can once again feel connected, praised, loved and safe.*

The Dependent

The *dependent* child ("child" includes teen years) also grows up feeling insecure and disconnected from his family and role models. The dependent child becomes a dishonest "people pleaser" to avoid confrontation, criticism and humiliation from the family controller(s). The dependent's inherited programming sends the crippling message, *"I am broken, unworthy and needy, and because of this feel great shame."* The dependent child attempts to escape his shame by being likeable, funny, charming, cool, smart and tough and survives by not "stirring the pot." The dependent child feels entitled to being rescued from his broken life. The dependent is "temporarily rescued" by the controller but then always returns to his "less than" default setting.

The dependent child's split from his root honesty and authentic self also creates obsessive-compulsive thinking and behavior. Out of loyalty, guilt and devotion, the dependent child continues to dishonestly "people please" so he won't feel disconnected and alone. The dependent child is forced to live in a dishonest world and learns to lie, manipulate and become *passive-aggressive* to get his needs met. The dependent's false definition of love becomes, *"I am loved because you rescue and enable me and I praise and honor you."* The dependent's definition of love is soon followed by rejection and abandonment. This becomes the revolving door pattern of the child dependent.

The following is an example of the dependent role. A female child-dependent and her controller mother. The child-dependent paints a picture that her controller mother loves and hangs on the wall for everyone to see. The "less than" child dependent now feels acceptance, love and a euphoric high connection with her mother. Later the child-dependent puts away her toys, and her controller mom suddenly criticizes her efforts in a harsh tone, *"Don't jam all of your toys in one box!"* The mother's voice communicates the message *"you can't do anything right."* The dependent child's euphoric bubble bursts and once again the dependent child returns to her shame based and "less than" default setting. The controller mom then correctly puts her daughters toys away in two boxes. *The mother's enabling is created from the controller's deep programmed fear that she must control, rescue and enable the dependent, so the dependent will survive and the controller will feel in control. The daughter learns, "I can't do it right so the controller must do it for me." Because both roles are unconscious, the mother may not even realize she has criticized her child and is also enabling her. The dependent child can only focus on "people pleasing" her mother to once again recreate their euphoric connection.*

Most of us don't like to think of ourselves as broken, needy, entitled, rescuing, enabling, over-controlling, dominating, etc. That is the point. These roles have nothing to do with our authentic self. The two codependent roles are assigned before birth, condition us (learned behavior) during child-teen years and destroy our emotional life, relationships and spiritual connection. I believe most of the general population inherits one of the codependent roles and gravitates (unconscious attraction) to the opposite role to create a codependent relationship. The controller will gravitate to the dependent and vice versa.

During a series of my workshops in a Los Angeles drug and alcohol treatment center, I discovered that most addicts inherit both

go

dependent and *controller* roles and unconsciously rotate between them.

Because the addict rotates between the two roles I have nicknamed addicts "rotators." One of the codependent roles will usually be dominant, the other will take a back seat position. At any time the back seat codependent role can rotate and become the dominant personality. Because both codependent roles are together in the addict's unconscious, they become extremely powerful and destructive. In the next chapter, Julian's story describes how his two inherited codependent roles (the controller and dependent) became his learned behavior during his child/teen years.

Chapter 2

Julian's Story - Childhood Codependence And Addiction

Julian's Story, *39-year-old male addict has been clean and sober for six years. Julian was in several of my counter-conditioning codependence and addiction workshops. Below is Julian's childhood codependence bio, which has been edited and shortened.*

I don't remember my father; he passed away two years after I was born. My first vivid memory in life was my grandparents' dog kennel filled with over one hundred wonderful small breed canines. I would spend my summer days playing, feeding and brushing them, preparing each one for his new home. It was sad to see them leave, but satisfying to know they were going to be a part of a new family and share their devoted love. There are a few lessons my canine pals taught me during my childhood. They loved me unconditionally. It didn't matter what I looked or smelled like, they were always ecstatic to see me. I have probably never experienced a more satisfying welcoming committee in my life. My grandparents' dogs showed me how to live in the present and express myself freely with uninhibited joy and happiness. My four-legged friends were loving and emotional creatures that wore their hearts on their paws. When I felt sad or lonely, I would sit with them and lose myself in their tongue-licking joy until I regained my sense of self. During this brief time, I felt a deep connection with people and nature. Life at my grandparents' kennel was magical and spontaneous, but soon everything would change.

When I was six years old, my mother remarried and my stepfather moved in with us. My stepfather was smart, charismatic and incredibly brutal. He quickly became my leader, my hero, my abuser. I looked up to him, loved him, feared him, worshiped him. He would build me up and then tear me down by criticizing and humiliating me until I felt completely numb over my entire body. It was at this time that I began to falsely perform to the outside world and then isolate with my inner voice, which I began to dislike. I soon started to experience a strange anxiety and nervous vibration in my thinking and behavior. I would later discover that the split from my true self created my life-long obsessive personality. The magical and uninhibited world at my grandparents' dog kennel slowly faded away.

By the time I was eight years old, I had learned to manipulate my stepfather to get my needs met. I became my stepfather's shadow, and felt entitled to have him take care of me. Most of the time I walked around with a poker face that said "I'm fine, I'm okay." I would rarely ask for anything. I spent most days living in my fantasy world, creating stories that would lift me above my deep emptiness and shame. I would constantly lie about my true feelings and obeyed my stepfather's guidance and domination. My self talk consisted of, *"I'm stupid, I'm nothing and my stepfather has the power to guide and control my life, and I desperately need him."* When my stepfather was not around, I became anxious and fearful. All my insecurities and anxieties would spin inside my head with nowhere to go. I felt lost and alone in the world without my step-father building me up, controlling me, and tearing me down.

Over time I developed a very strong radar for my stepfather's moods and temperament. If he were angry, I supported his anger, taking his side and defending his honor without questioning his motives. What happened in my outside world became my focus, and I would adjust, perform and lie to whomever or whatever the outside world wanted from me. My own inner voice and feelings became strangers I continued to disown. Most of the time I felt like a moving target, vulnerable and hypervigilant, always waiting for the proverbial rug to be pulled out from underneath me. My step-father's attention and acceptance became my main focus and obsession. The codependence between my stepfather and me was center stage, and all other relationships were superficially maintained and faded into the background. My job was to be the nicest and most likeable kid so no one would hurt me or question my passive aggressive behavior. When I hurt, lied and manipulated people, everyone would look the other way, not wanting to believe I was cruel or mean-spirited. It seemed the nicer I was the more I could get away with.

During my childhood and early teens, I started to notice that when my mind locked onto something, it wouldn't let go. If I wanted a bicycle, it would become my great obsession. I would go to the bicycle store several times a week and stare at it. I would collect pictures, draw pictures, talk about it, dream about it and beg my stepfather, mother and grandparents to buy me the bicycle. I would usually harass them daily until I got my way and they finally bought me the bicycle. After receiving the bike, I would spend most of my time riding it and then reach a quick burnout, get bored and abandon it. What I didn't realize was my relationship with the bicycle, my obsessive entitlement, the high of receiving it the quick burnout and abandonment were the beginning patterns of my addiction.

I believe sugar was my first drug of choice. I became a sugar junkie, buying and eating every sugar item sold at the local market. Carbonated drinks, candies, suckers, sugar cubes, anything that had sugar in it I would devour. My tongue was always a different candy-coated color. One of my favorite sugar treats were my grandmother's Jello boxes. I remember opening a box and licking my fingers and dabbing the powdered sugar several times during the day. One day, my grandmother found my stash of 37 empty Jello boxes hidden under my bed. She gently took my hand and looked into my eyes and lovingly said, "There's something wrong with you." She was right. Sugar tweaked and soothed my obsessive thinking but always left me wanting more.

When I was 11 years old, my mother and stepfather separated and divorced. I remember sitting with my grandparents' dogs, sobbing and completely devastated. My leader was leaving me and I was heartbroken and filled with fear. Even the fresh tongues of little puppies couldn't heal my grief, but after a few weeks I began to feel a great relief that my stepfather was gone. Being a dependent was exhausting and, as much as I missed his rescuing and leading me, I feared him and did not miss his shaming lectures and abuse.

Between the ages of 12 and 13 I experienced another shift and began my inherited controller role with my dependent mother. My mother has always needed a controller to take care of her, and when no controllers were around, it was my job. The transition from my own dependency issues to becoming a controller gave me a weird high and made me feel powerful and above my low self-esteem and depression. I didn't feel like a victim anymore, and believed I was a much nicer version of my stepfather with my mother. I was compassionate and understanding and believed I gave excellent advice on how my mother should live her life. When my mother was in a romantic relationship, there was usually conflict between her new boyfriend and myself. Two controllers trying to rescue, control and enable the same dependent doesn't work.

By the age of sixteen I had mastered both controller and dependent roles. The two codependent roles were in the foreground of all my relationships. If you were not a controller or dependent, I would lose interest in the relationship. Looking back, all my close friends were either a controller or a dependent. I did not choose them with this concept in mind; they were just my people and we clicked. During high school I acted cool and humble but was an arrogant, controlling know-it-all and became the relationship adviser for all my friends. I would talk and lecture them for hours on how to repair their relationships with boyfriends, girlfriends, family and loved ones. By the time I was 18, my prison of codependence had been created and was complete. I gradually began using more and more alcohol and drugs and had no idea I was hardwired to become a full blown alcoholic by the age of 24.

Julian's thinking and behavior as a dependent.

My emotional life became stuck, and I grew up with a broken, child-like immaturity.

I became sad and depressed because I disliked my inner voice.

I became extremely sensitive, defensive and on guard to my controller'(s) criticism, humiliation, moods, commands and controls.

I learned to be dishonest to survive, and I would say "yes" when I meant "no."

I apologized and said "I'm sorry" for things I was not responsible for.

I became passive-aggressive and manipulated people to get my needs met.

I was afraid to express my anger at the risk of being disliked.

My mind was prone to negative thinking, and it became nearly impossible to hold on to positive thoughts.

I always wanted more, believed I deserved more, and more was never enough.

Julian's thinking and behavior as a controller.

When I was fearful, I would obsessively attempt to over-control the thing I was afraid of, which created more anxiety.

I believed I had great insight and knew what was best for everyone.

I was domineering, bossy, opinionated and aggressive.

I was highly critical and judgmental.

I would give people solutions to their problems, even if they had not asked for them.

I became an angry victim when people did not do it my way.

I avoided and abandoned anyone I could not control or who would not do it my way.

I experienced a "high" while in control and rescuing someone and became anxious, like a craving drug addict, when there was no dependent to rescue and control.

The One Split Codependent

Most members of the world's population are one-split codependents who gravitate from their authentic selves to either the unconscious controller or dependent roles. You may, of course, be part of a very small percentage on the planet that did not inherit any codependence. The one-split codependent can usually function effectively in life and does not *rotate* the way addicts rotate. This does not mean he won't suffer innumerable disorders and illnesses created from codependence. I've known many one-split codependents who have built amazing careers but greatly suffer in their family and romantic relationships.

A one-split codependent can integrate his unconscious role with his core identity and superimpose a mix of root honesty and dishonesty that becomes very difficult to separate. The one-split codependent may never hit rock bottom or feel the need for professional help, not realizing he has inherited codependent behavior that is continually sabotaging and destroying his relationships. I believe the one-split codependent can experience *substance abuse* but not *full-blown addiction.* What one-split codependents can experience is the *illusion of addiction* when they gravitate and connect with another person in the opposite codependent role (either dependent or controller). The *illusion of addiction* or "temporary addiction" will end when the codependent relationship ends or the couple learns to set healthy boundaries.

A codependent who inherits the dependent role can be functional and successful. The dependent's embedded programming and *less than* default setting can seem almost non-existent. The dependent might be shy and introverted but has a positive and healthy self-esteem. When the dependent enters into a relationship with a controller, a shift into the dependent role's self-destructive programming can begin to take center stage. After the relationship's obsessive love bond and euphoric high sex, the dependent can begin to feel trapped in an argumentative power struggle and hostage situation instead of a balanced, loving relationship. The relationship's love bond and "euphoric high," cruelly transforms into a ball and chain of anxiety, emptiness, arguments and indifference. Unless the one-split codependent receives professional help and counter-conditions the codependent role, he most likely will gravitate into another codependent relationship and repeat the same pattern and behavior.

Later in this book, the one split can do the nine-step counter-conditioning process focusing on his one codependent role.

Chapter 3

The Destructive Addict's Loop

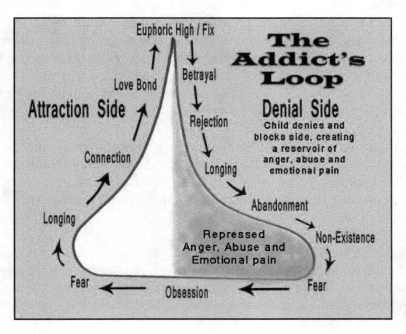

The controller child has been programmed to abandon himself and rescue and enable the dependent role. The dependent child has been programmed to abandon himself and be needy, broken and entitled, and needs a controller to rescue and enable him. The two codependent roles magnetically attract, creating a powerful biochemical "high" and revolving door pattern that I have named **THE ADDICT'S LOOP**.

Longing - Connection - Love Bond - Euphoric High/Fix - Betrayal - Rejection - Longing - Abandonment - Nonexistence

During a child's ("child" includes teen years) early conditioning, the left "attraction" side of the loop has the deception and illusion of a positive connection that creates an experience of feeling connected, safe and loved at the euphoric high/fix.

At some point, the right "denial" side of the loop reveals itself and *betrays, rejects and abandons.* This right side of the loop is psychologically blocked by the child's inability to process the overwhelming concept of being rejected and abandoned by his family and significant role models. Instead of confronting his rejection and abandonment, the child represses his *rejection, fear, abuse, anger and emotional pain,* which is stored in the loop's reservoir of denial (the unconscious). The repressed fear and emotional pain becomes an unidentifiable mass of pain and anxiety which the child learns to cope with.

As an example, a child on a roller coaster begins to go around the addict's loop. On the left "attraction" side of the addict's loop, the child obsesses and dishonestly performs his codependent role for his connection, love bond and euphoric high/fix in order to feel safe, accepted and loved.

After the roller coaster reaches the peak and creates its connection and euphoric high/fix, at some point it will continue down the right side of the addict's loop. The right, *denial side* of the loop suddenly reveals the child must now enter a *dark, scary tunnel* that represents *betrayal, rejection, abandonment and fear of nonexistence.* As the child enters the dark tunnel, he closes his eyes and denies the scary tunnel exists, longing to be reconnected at the euphoric high/fix. After leaving the scary tunnel, the child's fear, emotional pain and obsession fuels the child's journey back up through the left side of the loop to once again experience his *love bond, connection and euphoric high/fix.*

Let's look at another example and see how the addict's loop is created in a codependent relationship. The relationship is between a *controller* father and his young *dependent* son. One day, his dependent son becomes old enough to play Little League baseball. His controller father is a baseball fanatic and urges his son to sign up and be a pitcher for one of the teams. The dependent son doesn't like baseball but "people pleases" his controller father and signs up. The young dependent son rigorously practices every day with his father, who teaches him several pitching tricks and throws. During his first Little League game, the dependent son strikes out four players in a row and his team wins the game by several points. His controller father is ecstatic and hugs his son, buys him dinner and talks about his son possibly being a professional baseball player some day. The young dependent son feels a wonderful connection and euphoric high/fix with his controller father. His father has received him and treats him with admiration, love and respect.

Later that night while lying in bed, the young dependent son still feels extremely happy, "high" and elevated above his "less than" default setting. As the young dependent son lies in bed, he begins to worry and becomes fearful of letting his father down and of his father's disapproval, criticism and rejection. This creates feelings of *anxiety and fear mixed with euphoria*. The dependent son *represses* his fears and focuses on his euphoric high connection with his father.

The following week, the dependent son pitches another baseball game and walks six players in a row. He looks over at his father and sees him looking downward and shaking his head. Later in the game, the dependent son is at bat and hits a grounder into center field. The dependent son runs around the bases, trips and falls and is tagged out before arriving at third base. After the game, the boy's controller father walks ahead and ignores his dependent son and mutters, *"Hey, ya win some, ya lose some."* His young dependent son now feels disconnected, "less than" and heartbroken. The young dependent son represses his feelings of *rejection and abandonment* and can only focus on another way to win over his controller father and re-experience their connection and euphoric high/fix.

From the example above, on the left "attraction" side of the addict's loop the dependent son seeks to be received, loved and accepted by his controller father. When the dependent son strikes out four players in a row and wins the game, the dependent son feels a euphoric high/fix and a powerful connection with his controller father. This would complete the *attraction side* and euphoric high/fix on the left side of the addict's loop. During the son's euphoric high/fix he begins to fear disappointing his father and experiences waves of anxiety mixed with his euphoric high connection. The boy's fear and anxiety foreshadow what is about to happen on the right side of the addict's loop. In the following game, the dependent son walks six players, trips and falls and is tagged out before arriving at third base. His father's negative reaction reveals the dependent son's *betrayal, rejection and abandonment.* The dependent son does not analyze himself and think, *"I'm being rejected and abandoned by my father."* The dependent son simply cannot psychologically confront the concept of being *betrayed, rejected and abandoned* by his father. Instead he represses his fears of abandonment and races around the loop to the attraction side, seeking another way to feel connected with his father at the loop's euphoric high/fix.

The euphoric high/fix is an obsessive, self-centered blind spot that codependents and addicts obsessively gravitate toward and desperately attempt to control and manipulate in order to feel powerful, connected, loved and secure. The euphoric high/fix creates the temporary illusion of being elevated above the codependent and addict's feelings of powerlessness and shame to experience a womb-like wholeness. The codependent and addict blindly attempt to prove that the euphoric high/fix will some day magically transform and become unconditional love that lasts forever.

I use the word *nonexistence* on the addict's loop to describe the child's overwhelming and terrifying fear of being rejected and abandoned by family members or significant role models. Many codependent child and adult fears manifest themselves from the traumatizing and imaginary experience of *nonexistence* or fears of being "dropped off the cliff" if one does not feel received and connected at the loop's euphoric high/fix. In the addict's loop, the child will allow, protect and block unimaginable abuse that can lead to his own death to avoid the fear of *rejection and abandonment.* The child's unconscious message becomes, *"I must deny and repress my fear, abuse and painful feelings or I will be rejected and fall into the abyss of nothingness."* The more fear of abandonment a codependent child experiences, the more he will cling to the role(s), repress and deny his rejection, pain and abuse and seek salvation in the loop's euphoric high/fix.

The Addict's Loop and Unconscious Pain Load

Conscious Pain Load - The codependent's and addict's conscious awareness of abuse, emptiness, hopelessness, shame, guilt, remorse, despair, sadness, etc. These feelings and experiences are accessible and can be expressed and shared. *Using the baseball example, the young dependent son may feel sad he lost the game. He might talk to his mother about his feelings.*

Unconscious Pain Load - The codependent and addict's repressed and <u>unidentifiable</u> fears, disconnectedness, emotional pain, shame, guilt, rage, abuse and trauma stored in their unconscious or reservoir of denial in the addict's loop. *These are the painful feelings and fears of betrayal, rejection and abandonment the young baseball player repressed and blocked out.*

I'd like to add another concept to the baseball story. Later that day, after the dependent son walks six players and loses the baseball game, his father is organizing his son's baseball bag. The young boy approaches his father with his baseball mitt and places it in the sports bag. The father grabs the mitt and throws it at his son, hitting him in the face. The young boy starts to cry and the father says, *"Sorry! We need to practice!"* The young boy stops crying, wipes his eyes and watches his controller father finish organizing his baseball equipment. The boy's abuse (by accident or on purpose) also becomes repressed in the addict's loop reservoir of denial. The dependent son is already programmed to believe he is "less than" and a failure. When his father throws the mitt in his face, the boy thinks *"I failed my father and I deserved that."* The young boy continues to repress his *rejection, abandonment, emotional pain and abuse (unconscious pain load),* which slowly begins to grow and rise like a hot air balloon toward consciousness.

As the reservoir in the addict's loop stacks and fills with repressed and unidentifiable *rejection, abandonment, anger, abuse and emotional pain,* it creates unidentifiable *waves of pain and anxiety* that attempt to surface into consciousness. As the child revolves around the addict's loop, he recreates more and more of his unconscious pain load. Over the years, the child creates a high tolerance to his unconscious pain load by continually repressing and denying it. The child and adult codependent will attempt to numb and escape their rising and ballooning unconscious pain load with *sugar, food, video games, alcohol, drugs, etc.*

The Codependent Child's Emotional Life On The Addict's Loop

The dependent is programmed and conditioned to repress and deny his anger, not wanting to be a problem. When the dependent does express anger, he usually goes from calm to rage in a few seconds. The dependent will usually build and repress his anger over a long period of time until he finally explodes. The dependent can feel extremely guilty and shameful after he vents his anger and may become depressed, the unconscious and destructive message being *"you're now a problem and you've just become unlovable."* To avoid being a problem, the dependent will usually pass his pain load *passive aggressively*. The child controller will usually believe he does not deserve the pain load and will fight with his parents, friends and role models and vent his deep emotional pain. Families may work through relationship issues and conflicts, but codependence is under the family radar and is rarely identified. The controller child and family may develop a compassionate understanding of each other, but codependent patterns will continue to unconsciously sabotage the child's present and future relationships unless they are uncovered and treated.

Before leaving home, a child may revolve around the addict's loop thousands of times. The child's emotional life is greatly damaged by his codependent split(s) and the roller coaster progression of the addict's loop. Revolving around the loop creates a broken message that love is always conditional, which leaves the child empty and defeated. The child's internal message becomes, *"If I'm not the best, I won't add up, be good enough or loveable."* When the child experiences being accepted, the feelings of doom may immediately follow, the internal message being *"You can't trust love because it* won't last," and, *"I can't make this work, I must be broken and defective."*

The example is in the baseball story, when the dependent boy is laying in bed feeling a "euphoric high" connection but also experiencing fear and anxiety from his father's potential criticism, rejection and emotional abandonment. The young boy's emotional radar of predicting and fearing failure and feeling "less than" and being humiliated becomes a built-in reaction to anything positive. At some point, the child's euphoric high/fix connection to feel loved and accepted by his controller father will be trumped by his rising, unconscious pain load. For example, later in his early teens, the dependent baseball player has repressed so much *betrayal, rejection, abandonment, emotional pain and abuse* it destroys any desire to be connected with his controller father. The young boy's euphoric high/fix has completely flat-lined. Instead of wanting to feel connected and loved by his father, the boy resents him and isolates. During this pain load peak, the child-teen can feel emotionally numb and disconnected from himself and his family's emotional life. The child's overwhelming pain load peak can detach him into self-destructive behavior, substance abuse, addiction and possibly suicide.

Let's review the baseball story from the perspective of the controller father. I don't want to make the controller always "the bad guy." From the controller father's point of view, he fears for his son's survival. He sees his son having potential but always witnesses his dependent son stumbling, falling short and failing. The controller father's inner voice tells him, *"I try to help my son but he always sabotages his own efforts and becomes defeated, broken and weak. I fear the world will eat him up and spit him out."* This constant fear in the controller role makes the father demanding and he pushes harder. When the dependent son falls short and fails, the father's fears are triggered and he sends a gesture or verbal message of disappointment. The controller's own belief is, *"If he were more like me, I wouldn't have to fear for his survival."* Over several years of witnessing his son's self-defeating behavior, the controller father starts to believe his dependent son is failing just to hurt and spite him.

Let's revisit the abuse that happened when the controller father threw the baseball mitt and hit his son's face. Instead of the father throwing the mitt, let's turn the abuse around. Over several months, the dependent son has repressed his *betrayal, rejection and abandonment* from the codependent relationship with his controller father. The dependent son's repressed anger and rage finally surface. The boy suddenly screams, *"I hate baseball!"* The young dependent son throws a baseball and hits his father in the head. The young boy runs off crying and his controller father represses the abuse because he feels guilty and defeated for losing control of the relationship. He blames himself for being too hard on his dependent son. The father then says to himself, *"I try so hard to help my son succeed and all I get is a baseball thrown at my head."* The controller father ends up abandoned and a victim of his dependent son's rejection, anger and abuse.

Transitioning From Child To Teen/Adult Codependent Relationships

As the dependent child becomes a teen/adult, he will usually gravitate to a controller for his intimate relationships. A controller adult will usually gravitate to a dependent. These relationships attract with the obsessive power of a drug addiction, creating a euphoric high/fix connection and biochemical high attraction. For example, on the left, *attraction side* of the addict's loop, the dependent and controller have a powerful sexual connection. The dependent is programmed to be rescued and enabled by the controller. The controller feels deeply loved and worshiped for "running the show" and being the beacon of light and "magic helper." The controller and dependent can experience the illusion of love at first sight and finding their soul mates.

Entering the right, *denial side* of the addict's loop, the dependent *at* some point is revealed and seen as broken, emotionally immature and irresponsible in many areas of life. The controller becomes resentful for carrying the relationship responsibility. The dependent's entitlement, selfishness and neediness progresses, and the controller becomes critical and judgmental. The dependent resents the controller's criticism, lectures and control, so he isolates. The controller feels betrayed and rejected and becomes a hurt and angry victim. The relationship's obsessive sexual connection and magic love bond and euphoria are gradually dominated and destroyed by the right side of the addict's loop -- *betrayal, rejection and abandonment.*

The addict's loop creates confusion and heartbreak in relationships. The attraction side of the loop makes the codependents feel they are the most desirable partners on the planet. As the loop progresses into the denial side, *betrayal, rejection and abandonment,* the codependents begin to feel unworthy, unattractive and undesirable, the cruel and heartbreaking message being, *"I was everything to my partner and now I'm nothing."* Ironically, when the relationship ends, each codependent can experience the strange and empty feeling of, *"What was I doing with that person?"* Someone who shared a powerful and intimate connection is now looked upon as a complete stranger. Codependents are powerfully attracted and then become "objects" who perform their unconscious roles, creating a confusing and conflicting message of, *"I'm obsessed and attracted to this person but feel angry, disconnected, fearful and lonely in the relationship."*

During the relationship, any abuse from the denial side of the addict's loop can be blocked and experienced as something new and a complete surprise each time it occurs. For example, a wife says to her friend, *"He was so sweet and loving, and then I asked about his job search and he screamed and threw a lamp at me! I can't believe he's so nasty and violent!"*

A friend witnessing their relationship might observe the wife complaining about her husband's violence several times in the past few weeks, but each time the wife reacts as if her husband's violent temper is something completely new. This powerful denial was created when the child was conditioned to block out *the dark, scary tunnel of abuse and abandonment* on the right side of the addict's loop. Any emotional, physical or sexual abuse blocked in the dark scary tunnel may surface and blindly recreate itself in the present day relationship. Emotional, physical and sexual abuse between the controller and dependent will usually be covert and secretly protected. Because the relationship is blinded by a false definition of love, both roles can receive abuse and believe it's their own fault. The dependent will receive the abuse and believe he deserves or promoted the abuse, and the controller can receive the abuse and believe it's his fault for losing control of the relationship. Because of this dynamic, the abuse stays repressed and protected and continues in the relationship and future relationships.

Also, any abuse that is repressed and protected in the codependent relationship can become connected to the loop's euphoric high/fix. A child who has been emotionally, physically and/or sexually abused can later, in his adult relationships, unconsciously enmesh the abuse as a "fix" and recreate the abuse to feel connected and loved in the codependent relationship. The conflicting and destructive unconscious message becomes, *"To feel connected and loved, I must experience being abused."* Because the addict's loop is progressive, the abuse can also progress and finally destroy the relationship and/or codependent.

For example, you were a dependent daughter to your controller father. Your father abused you. On the right denial side of the addict's loop, you unconsciously repressed and blocked out the abuse and performed the dependent's "people pleasing" role so you wouldn't feel rejected and abandoned. *Remember, the child will tolerate unimaginable abuse in order to not feel abandoned and fall into the abyss of non-existence.* Later, in a romantic relationship, you have a powerful, passionate and euphoric connection with your male partner that later becomes abusive. You feel betrayed, heartbroken, shameful and angry but continue to stay in the relationship hoping your partner will magically awaken, stop abusing you and love you forever. These are the same feelings and abuse you repressed during your childhood experience with your father; hopeful, heartbroken, filled with shame and anger, hoping someday your father would awaken, stop abusing you and love you forever. The dependent and controller become trapped in a relationship by two powerful, unconscious messages, *"If the relationship ends, I'll be rejected and abandoned into non-existence,"* and the dependent's repressed hopes and dreams of the abusive father and partner magically awakening and loving her forever in the union of the euphoric high/fix. These two powerful unconscious messages keep the codependent attached to the progressive and destructive relationship.

The same crippling message can be experienced with the abusive controller in the relationship. The abusive controller father also recreates his own repressed abuse which he experienced and blocked during his childhood years in the dark scary tunnel and denial side of the addict's loop. The unconscious destructive message becomes, *"To feel connected and in control, I must abuse the one I love."* This is not a conscious thought or behavior, but the controller's own repressed abuse, entangled and blindly enmeshed in his codependent relationship and euphoric high/fix on the addict's loop.

I'd like to do a visualization of the addict's loop. After reading the following sentences, close your eyes and imagine the addict's loop in your mind's eye. On the left side of the addict's loop is the "attraction side" that moves toward the tip of the loop's euphoric high/fix. On the attraction side, both codependent roles want to fulfill their programming and feel successful, connected and loved. The dependent role dishonestly "people pleases" (I'll be anything you want) to feel loved and rescued by the controller. The controller wants to rescue the dependent (do as I say and you'll survive) and feel powerful, praised and loved. When the two roles complete their union, they experience the euphoric high/fix. *In the baseball story, this was when the dependent son struck out four players in a row, won the game and became adored, respected and loved by his controller father.* Close your eyes and focus on one of the codependent roles wanting to fulfill and connect with the opposite codependent role to experience the loop's euphoric high/fix. Personally, I can feel my body chemistry change and begin to feel "high."

Now, let's visualize the right "denial side" of the addict's loop. The denial side represents the *betrayal, rejection and abandonment and the fear of nonexistence.* Now, think of each role repelling the other. The dependent "screws up" and is criticized by the controller and isolates and goes back into his shell and is alone. The controller feels like a failure because his control and directions have failed and the dependent has rejected and abandoned him. The controller now feels like a victim and is also alone. The "denial side" of the loop is where both codependent roles repress their *betrayal, rejection, abandonment and any abuse.* It is nearly impossible for a child to experience these powerful words and experiences that condemn him to being abandoned, disconnected and the imaginary fear of *nonexistence.* During our childhood, we did everything possible to avoid being *betrayed, rejected and abandoned.* Some of us were loved and nurtured but still never felt good enough. Some of us were humiliated, slapped, punched, beaten and molested. We had to repress the abuse and painful feelings to survive and feel connected and loved, even if it was a fantasy. Now, see yourself repressing these painful feelings over and over. As you repress these painful feelings and experiences, visualize them stacking and building up inside the loop's reservoir of denial. Now visualize your painful feelings rising toward the euphoric high/fix and finally over powering and destroying it.

Close your eyes one more time and see the entire addict's loop. Visualize yourself going up the attraction side to feel received and loved at the euphoric high/fix and then suddenly falling into the denial side and repressing your *abuse, betrayal, rejection and abandonment.* Visualize yourself filled with anxiety and fear and moving around the loop toward the attraction side to once again feel connected at the euphoric high/fix.

Let's review the addict's loop and look at its built-in mechanics hidden in the unconscious. Every time I experience the euphoric high/fix, at some point, I will also experience *betrayal, rejection and abandonment.* The addict's loop has programmed me to block and repress my *emotional pain, betrayal, rejection, abandonment and any abuse* which creates a stacking and layering effect that slowly rises and fills up the loop's reservoir of denial. The repressed and ballooning unidentifiable pain load creates fear and anxiety and makes me need more euphoric high/fix to numb and escape. See the insanity? The addict's loop is designed and creates *a self-drowning effect.* The more I experience the euphoric high/fix, the more fear and pain I create and repress, which stacks and rises toward consciousness, and then I need more euphoric high/fix to once again escape. At some point, the repressed, unidentifiable pain load surfaces and dominates the euphoric high/fix and completely flatlines the emotional life of the codependent and addict.

Substance Abuse

During the codependent relationship, the dependent may compulsively use *alcohol, drugs, gambling, food, sex, etc.* The substance abuse and behavior can create *the illusion of addiction.* During a codependent relationship the dependent can self-medicate, numb and escape the right side of the loop's *repressed abuse and fear of betrayal, rejection and abandonment* that continually attempts to recreate itself and surface during the relationship.

An example of *substance abuse* and *temporary addiction* or the *illusion of addiction* is that as the dependent recreates her unconscious pain load and re-experiences *betrayal, rejection, abandonment and any possible abuse* in her adult relationship, the dependent might begin to use food to numb her surfacing unconscious pain load on the addict's loop. The dependent slowly loses control and compulsively snacks to escape and numb the surfacing pain load and progressively gains weight. The dependent may think she's a food addict and even seek professional help and treatment. Once the relationship ends or the dependent learns to set healthy boundaries, the dependent will discover she can regain control over food and return to her normal weight. The addict's loop that is created between the codependent relationship *idles* and loses its power after adjustments are made or the relationship ends.

Another example of substance abuse that can look like addiction is a male dependent who drinks alcohol and smokes pot everyday. Let's say the dependent has been married to a controller for twenty years. The dependent has used alcohol and pot during the marriage to self-medicate his rising, unconscious pain load recreated from the addict's loop and codependent relationship. The difference between addiction and abuse is the substance use will not progress and completely dominant and destroy the dependent's life. The dependent might binge and be a heavy user but can still function in his life. I want to make it clear that substance abuse can kill someone, they can OD or die from years of wear and tear and the effects of drugs and alcohol on their body and mind. The point is, at some point substance abuse can be completely controlled and end. Addiction continues in the addict's unconscious and can be managed but does not end. This is why it is crucial the addict learns to stay out of the behavior of both inherited codependent roles.

The Seven Stages Of An Intimate Codependent Relationship

Codependent relationships can be extremely deceiving and make a person feel broken and unlovable. Simply put, every time the addict's loop embraces you with its euphoric high/fix, it will throw you off the rocky cliff to the jagged shoreline below. I have outlined below the seven stages of an intimate and obsessive codependent relationship which behaves and progresses like a drug addiction.

Highlight any sentences below you personally relate to in the seven stages of an intimate codependent relationship.

Stages 1-3 represent the left "attraction" side of the addict's loop ... Longing - Connection - Love Bond - Euphoric High/Fix

Stage 1 - The drug has two legs

A magnetic attraction, the illusion of "love at first sight" and finding your soul mate are experienced by the couple. The relationship becomes accelerated and obsessive. Many phone calls and text messages are shared a number of times a day. There is an overwhelming desire, obsession, fear and anxiety to be with each other. Romantic and sexual relationships are intense and compulsive. There are premature, obsessive thoughts of a future together and a heightened fear of rejection and abandonment before and during the relationship.

Stage 2 - Rolling the joint, cutting the cocaine, heating the heroin

The dependent can be extremely charming, cool, intelligent, funny and talented. The dependent will unconsciously use heartbreaking history as bait and grooms the controller to take care of him. The dependent will share personal history of emotional abuse, physical abuse, sexual abuse, abandonment, family deaths and suicides. The dependent will also talk about broken romantic relationships and how he was a victim of love. The controller connects and relates to the trauma-bond intimacy. The controller feels concern and pity for dependent's survival. The controller feels love can heal the dependent from his heartbreaking past and help him fulfill his hidden potential. The hook has been set for the controller to take care of the dependent. The dependent may have sufficient financial resources but still needs the controller to carry his emotional life.

Stage 3 - Doing the drug and the euphoric high/fix

The relationship moves quickly, and the controller and dependent will usually begin to live together within a short time. The couple is inseparable and do most things together. The relationship and sex feel like a powerful euphoric drug "high." There's an innocent stalking and worrying whether the other person is okay. If one does not check in at a certain time, it can create obsessive fear and anxiety. All negative aspects of each other are in denial and many excuses are made for each others shortcomings.

Stages 4-7 represent the right "denial" side of the addict's loop... Betrayal - Rejection - Longing - Abandonment – Nonexistence

Stage 4 - Coming down off the drug

The controller sooner or later becomes aware that she is carrying most, if not all of the responsibility in the relationship. The controller becomes a lecturing parent and the dependent becomes an entitled and irresponsible, broken child. The controller takes care of most of dependent's life choices and makes many decisions. The dependent listens to the controller's directions and seems to understand, but deep inside the dependent is programmed to be broken and rarely changes his behavior. Frustration builds, and relationship starts to become unglued. The dependent feels self-conscious, exposed and humiliated, becomes angry, withdraws and gives love crumbs. The controller feels rejected, angry and hurt and continues exposing the dependent's inability to be responsible, loving and supportive. Sex life fades.

Stage 5 - The relationship becomes a bad hangover

Manipulation, anger, hurt, rejection, loneliness and pain become the core of the relationship. The dependent sees the controller as nagging and domineering. The controller sees dependent as lazy, entitled, manipulating, selfish and dishonest. Fighting, arguing and possible abuse become the main event of the relationship. Both the controller and dependent start fantasizing about other relationships and possibly begin having affairs. Both can fantasize about partner dying. Stages four and five can also become chronic and last for many years. Over several years, the dependent can completely lose himself "people pleasing," becoming deeply enmeshed in and beginning to mirror the controller's personality and belief system. The relationship becomes a revolving door of frustration, misery, anger and heartbreak.

Stage 6 - Out of drugs, desperate, and craving to reconnect

Affairs, abandonment, betrayal, rejection, anger, rage, emotional abuse, physical abuse, restraining orders, arrests, homicide and suicide can occur. To avoid abandonment, each codependent will desperately try to reconnect and recreate the euphoric high/fix. Stage six can be the most dangerous and destructive of the seven stages. Behind the controller or dependent's repressed fears of abandonment can be an unknown source of destructive rage, directed toward the partner and self.

Stage 7 - A junkie on the hunt, chasing the dragon

The dependent or controller may return to the relationship and shower partner with love and promise that things will be different this time. The relationship may resume several times, but the unconscious addict's loop will continue to progress and destroy the relationship. The relationship finally ends and the revolving door of codependence and the addict's loop seeks a new partner to repeat its destructive pattern.

Chapter 4

Addiction

Placed in the addict's unconscious is the addicts loop, which is created from the two inherited codependent roles. The addict's loop creates the addict's "high" and progressive addiction. The euphoric high/fix or addict's "high" is temporary. At some point, the addict's drug of choice dissipates and ends but the addict's fears, shame, powerlessness and pain is repressed and each time is recreated inside the loop's reservoir of denial. Over and over, the addict is tricked and deceived by the loops unconscious mechanics and temporary "high." The euphoric high/fix psychologically blinds the addict and creates the illusion of feeling complete, in control and whole. As the addict enters the denial side of the loop and comes down off his "high," he unconsciously adds, rebuilds, stacks and enlarges his fears, shame and pain. The addict's loop becomes an unconscious pain making mechanism. The analogy is pouring gasoline on a fire, believing every time the gasoline will put the fire out.

To understand addiction, visualize the controller role and dependent role, positioned across from each other in the addict's unconscious. Both roles idle and create the dependent's embedded and programmed "less than" shame and the controller's loss of control and powerlessness. These become the main two psychological triggers that motivate the addict's internal rescue mission. Because both roles are in the unconscious, they're permanently separated and cannot connect and rescue each other unless there is a catalyst. The catalyst is the addict's euphoric "fix" (alcohol, drugs, sex, gambling, etc.), that temporarily merges and fulfills the addict's internal "rescue mission," between his two codependent roles. During the addict's substance use, the dependent is transformed and feels connected, rescued and safe and the controller feels powerful, bigger than life and in control. At the peak of the addict's internal rescue mission is the euphoric high/fix on the addict's loop. The addict's internal rescue mission and "high" is only a "temporary fix." When the addict's drug of choice ends, both codependent roles reawaken and discover, once again, they're disconnected, abandoned, separated and alone in the addict's unconscious. The dependent, once again, feels "less than" and the controller feels a loss of control and powerlessness. This awareness triggers the addict to seek the euphoric high/fix on the addict's loop and recreate the internal rescue mission between his two codependent roles.

During childhood years, the addict unconsciously learns to self-contaminate and abandon his root honesty and core identity. I have named this unconscious process *echo shaming*. The shift out of the addict's authentic self into both codependent roles creates a chronic disconnectedness and incompleteness. The emotional pain of always being on the "other side of the aquarium glass" unconsciously gravitates the addict to seek the euphoric high/fix, which creates the temporary illusion and self rescue mission to feel whole, in control and elevated above his pain load and "less than" default setting. Even when the addict celebrates and is happy, he unconsciously experiences a deep disconnectedness and anxiety from his two codependent splits, which gravitates the addict to seek wholeness through his arsenal of fixes. As the addict seeks the euphoric high/fix, any consequences or damage control will be blocked by the denial side of the addict's loop. This is why an addict won't pause before taking a hit off a crack pipe and think, *"If I smoke this, it'll destroy three hundred million brain cells and possibly kill me."* The addict is psychologically blinded by the euphoric high/fix on the addict's loop, until he re-awakens into the denial side of his *hangover, rejection, abandonment, remorse, guilt and shame.* Basically, the addict can only experience the feel good "high" on the addict's loop and not the bad stuff (hangover), waiting on the blocked denial side of the addict's loop. Every time the addict fixes, more repressed fear and pain is recreated and stored in the loop's reservoir of denial and attempts to surface into consciousness. The addict straight-arms the unidentifiable, rising pain load with more substance and behavior fixes. This becomes the progressive and destructive revolving door pattern of the addict's loop, centered in the addict's unconscious.

In the core of unconscious addiction is the dependent's inherited and programmed *entitlement,* and the controller's inherited and programmed *enabling.* This connection point is where unconscious addiction progresses and destroys. The great illusion of both codependent roles occurs because the controller believes his power can control, rescue and satisfy the dependent's entitlement and the dependent believes the controller's power and enabling will finally heal his disconnectedness, shame and "less than" default setting. Behind the blinding light of the euphoric high/fix hides the addict's bottomless black hole, where the controller can never satisfy the dependent's entitlement and the dependent can never be rescued and saved. In the beginning, both roles truly believe they can satisfy and complete their mission of rescuing and being rescued. Both codependent roles start out hopeful and exercise control and choice and then are betrayed each time at the euphoric high/fix and lose control and fall into the denial side and bottomless pit of the addict's loop.

It is my belief that whenever the addict's internal dependent role is triggered by his fear, shame and "less than" feelings or the addict's internal controller role feels powerless and a loss of control, the addict seeks a *euphoric fix* to create the union between the two unconscious codependent roles. Basically, behind the addict's substance use and behavior is an unconscious self rescue mission. Within the addict's "high" the dependent will be rescued and saved from his "less than" and shame based default setting and the controller will become powerful, in control, praised and worshipped. This becomes the addict's temporary "high" and why the addict's substance and behavior fixes are powerfully centered in the addict's life, until his drug of choice completely *betrays, rejects and abandons.* From this dynamic, two powerful triggers are created. Whenever the dependent role feels "less than" and the controller role feels they're losing their power and control, the addict seeks a "fix" to recreate his internal rescue mission between his two codependent roles. Many addicts, after bottoming out from substance use, will express the painful feeling that *"their lover has turned on them."* Symbolically, it has done exactly that, and it continues to play out the multi-generational roles of the broken, needy and entitled dependent and the rescuing, enabling and powerful controller, seeking their internal rescue mission with addiction fixes, to create the euphoric high/fix on the addict's loop.

It is also my belief that child and teen *rotators* can have a number of other co-occurring illnesses and mental disorders that have been conditioned and passed down through their multi-generational family tree. Many disorders like bipolar, ADD, ADHD and several other chronic disorders may be directly related to the inherited codependent split(s), addict's loop and chronic rotation and abuse that has reoccurred over several generations and is inherited and reconditioned in the present generation. At their core, many of the cyclical disorders and illnesses mimic the extreme highs and lows and destructive attachment-abandonment trauma created by the progressive addict's loop. For example, bipolar disorder. Over several generations, the bipolar depression or "low" could be created from the shame based, "less than" dependent role and the bipolar manic side from the powerful and rescuing controller role.

Many addicts come from loving homes and have not experienced any abuse or trauma. In a loving house of addiction and codependence, the family or central role models can be successful, nurturing and functional. There may be no signs of addiction with any relatives, past or present. In this loving house of addiction, codependence is a covert blind spot that can be passed to the next generation. I've had many addicts in my workshops who come from loving homes, were never abused, and discovered during the workshop and writing exercises that they *rotated both codependent roles* and have always felt a deep disconnectedness, powerlessness and unworthiness. Many addicts from a nurturing home environment feel guilty and shameful for not being functional and successful like some of their family members and relatives. The constant reminder of not being good enough triggers the dependent's "less than" default setting and the controller's rise to power, which fuels the addicts drug of choice and recreates the addict's revolving, internal rescue mission between his two codependent roles.

Substance *abuse* can completely destroy and end someone's life. Substance *abuse* at some point can be controlled. Addiction progresses, and at some point the addict loses complete control.

There are many bio-psycho-social-spiritual and co-occurring disorders and illnesses that can compound substance and behavioral *abuse* and *addiction.* My addiction model simply shows that, when you strip it all down, the addict's loop is the main driving force behind addiction. An addict can come from a loving home where there has been no abuse or history of addiction. The addict has no co-occurring disorders or illnesses, is healthy, financially secure, successful, and has a loving (codependent) family and support system. When you subtract and take away all the bio-psycho-social-spiritual issues and co occurring disorders and illnesses that can compound addiction, the addict will be left standing with both unconscious codependent roles, be a *rotator,* and lose complete control of his substance use and life.

The Biochemical Loop

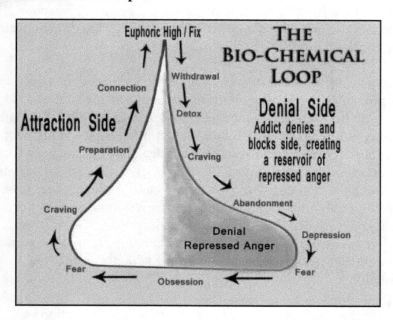

For thousands of years, the addict's loop of ...

Longing - Connection - Love Bond - Euphoric High/Fix - Betrayal - Rejection - Longing - Abandonment - Nonexistence

... has been unconsciously communicated to the human biology and has created an analogous biochemical loop of ...

Craving - Preparation - Connection - Euphoric High/Fix - Withdrawal - Detox - Craving - Abandonment - Depression

The addict's biochemical loop creates a similar obsessive attraction side for his drug of choice. The attraction side creates *craving, preparation, connection and euphoric high/fix.* On the addict's loop and attraction side, the codependent child obsesses and longs to feel connected and loved at the euphoric high/fix.

The addict on the biochemical loop also blocks out the right denial side of *withdrawal, detox, craving, abandonment and depression (the addict's hangover) and craves to be reconnected at the euphoric high/fix.* The codependent child on the addict's loop blocks out the right denial side of the loop's *betrayal, rejection, abandonment and fear of nonexistence* and longs to be reconnected at the euphoric high/fix.

It's easy to see the similarity in both loops. The addict can only see and experience the blinding light of the euphoric high/fix and cannot see his *hangover, detox, depression* until he reawakens into it, which motivates him to escape back into the euphoric high/fix. The codependent child can only experience his euphoric high/fix to feel connected, safe and loved and cannot experience the *betrayal, rejection and abandonment*, which he blocks, denies and represses. He then quickly moves around the loop to feel connected again at the euphoric high/fix. When the addict's loop connects with the inherited biochemical loop, an addict is created. Both loops work in tandem and feed each other toward the addict's complete destruction.

Let's use the baseball story again to describe how addiction is created and fueled with both the addict's loop and biochemical loop in a relationship. Jumping years ahead in the baseball story, the young dependent boy is now a teenager and experiences a shift from his dependent role into his controller role (similar to Julian's story in chapter 2). The teenager has inherited both codependent roles. The teenager has the "less than" dependent role and also the powerful, rescuing and enabling controller role. The teenager *rotates* between the two roles in his surrounding relationships. Let's say, the teenager has a big final test coming up and his controller father helps him study and prepare. The teenager gets a C+ on the test and once again see's that his controller father is very disappointed.

Instead of the teenager trying to win his father's love and acceptance and recreate their euphoric high/fix, he buys some *methamphetamine* and creates his own euphoric high/fix with the drug between his own internal dependent and controller roles. Both the addict's loop and biochemical loop kick into gear. The *meth* has replaced the teenager's rescuing and controlling father and their euphoric high/fix on the addict's loop. Unconsciously, the teenager replaces his father's controller role with his own internal controller role and *meth*. The *meth* becomes the euphoric catalyst, rescuing his own dependent role's "less than" and shame based default setting and elevates his internal controller role to feel powerful and in control. The teenager has recreated the euphoric high/fix in himself and feels above his pain, in control and whole. Because the teenager cannot see his "hangover" or any negative consequences (blocked out on the right side of both loops), he continues to experience and use *meth* as his new personal savior, rescuer and best friend.

The controller father feels disconnected and abandoned by his addict son. The addict son has replace his father with *meth* and no longer needs the euphoric connection with his father. The controller father and his addict son begin to feel like two complete strangers living under the same roof. Over time, the teenage son becomes more dependent on *meth* to recreate the unconscious rescue mission of his two internal codependent roles. Both the addict's loop and biochemical loop creates a self-drowning effect. The biochemical loop creates a similar withdrawal, craving and tolerance. The more *meth* the teenager uses, the more he needs to get "high." The more he gets "high" the more repressed pain he recreates, which attempts to surface into consciousness and the teenager needs more *meth* to escape. The teenage son begins to lose control and feels shameful and "less than" that he cannot control his *meth* use. This fuels more *meth* use to feel powerful and in control. As the teenager's addiction progresses, his two codependent roles become amplified and bigger than life. The dependent becomes extremely needy and broken and the controller becomes manic, over the top and desperate to regain control. The controller father sees that his son's life is in great danger and that his son needs more and more *meth* to save himself. For the purpose of this story, the father enables his son's addiction. The controller father begins to look the other way and may even buy his son *meth*.

Unconsciously, the controller father accepts he's been replaced by the drug and will assist supplying his son with his replacement, the *meth*, a symbol of his own rescuing and enabling controller role. The father attempts to control his son's addiction and his son completely isolates into his own internal codependent roles that recreate his self-rescue mission. The father finally awakens and realizes his enabling is assisting in his son's complete destruction. The controller father takes his son to a drug treatment center. It is important to mention that it is not the father's fault that his son has addiction. His son inherited both codependent roles and the biochemical loop. The father did not give his son the two codependent roles and the biochemical loop. What the father does is enable and fuel his son's *meth* use. The father must learn to counter-condition his own controller role, which fuels his son's addiction.

Let's jump ahead, and now the teenage addict is an adult. The addict gravitates to a female controller and together they create a codependent relationship. In the beginning of the relationship (attraction, connection, love bond and euphoric high/fix), the addict may not have any desire to use *meth* because the codependent relationship and sex are creating the euphoric high/fix. The addict feels whole, loved and connected in the relationship that creates a powerful union. When the relationship begins to unravel and move into the right side of the addict's loop, *betrayal, rejection and abandonment,* the addict's dependent role is exposed by his controller girlfriend as entitled, broken, selfish and needy. The addict shuts down and emotionally abandons and isolates from his controller girlfriend and uses *meth* to recreate his own internal rescue mission between his unconscious dependent and controller roles. Once again, the addict's two unconscious roles become dependent on the addict's drug of choice to recreate his self rescue mission.

The Powerful Addiction Pathway

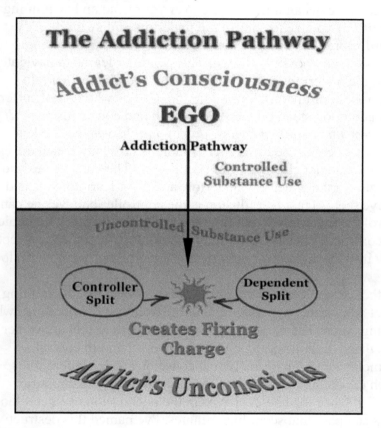

The internal rescue mission and connection of the two codependent roles creates the addiction pathway that transitions the addict's conscious control into his unconscious addict's loop and euphoric high/fix. As the addict continues substance use, his conscious control is weakened. The addict's substance and/or behavioral *fixes* create a reverse effect and strengthen the unconscious pathway and euphoric high/fix (fixing charge in graphic).

An analogy that could describe the addict's loss of control and addiction pathway is the undertow at the beach. Imagine standing in the ocean and not realizing there is an undertow beneath you. You are twenty feet from the shore watching the waves break, and when you look back at the shore, you are now thirty feet. You watch the waves, turn around, and now you are forty feet. Every time you turn and look at the shore, you are magically further and deeper in the ocean until you are over your head and swimming for your life. If you try to control the undertow and swim directly toward shore you will be carried even further away, become exhausted, and possibly drown. The swimmer learns to navigate out of the undertow, just as I believe the addict must learn to navigate out of unconscious addiction. Critics who do not suffer from addiction stand on the sandy beach and constantly say, *"If you know there's an undertow, don't go in the water."* Makes perfect sense, but the difference is there is no sandy beach on which the addict can anchor his willpower. The addict lives and struggles in the water and undertow and must learn to cope and survive there. The great illusion is the controller believes he can control the undertow. Each time the controller begins with choice and control of his substance and behavioral *fix* and then is swept away into the addiction pathway and undertow of the addict's loop.

Another example of the addiction pathway could be a gambling addict who seems hypnotically cut off from her surroundings when playing cards. The addict's unconscious desire to feel above her "less than" default setting and feel powerful and in control summons the union of the two unconscious codependent roles, which create the pathway into the addict's loop and euphoric high/fix. Once the addict arrives in the unconscious addict's loop, hours can pass that seem like minutes. I've named this destructive and unconscious zone where the addict's loop lives and destroys, the "land of the fix."

The same effect can happen when the addict uses substances. During the addict's third drink, or "hit," she begins the transition from conscious control into the addiction pathway, then into the addict's loop and euphoric high/fix. *Remember, the addict's controller role always believes she can control her "fix."* As the addict transitions into the unconscious addict's loop, the fueling system and revolving door pattern of both loops begin to control and weaken the addict's awareness and control. The addict's loop creates the undertow into the addict's unconscious *land of the fix* where the addict loses complete control and hours can pass that seem like minutes.

The following example describes how the addict's loop works with *thoughts and feelings.* An addict is washing dishes in his kitchen. The addict's "less than" default setting and depression begins to create anxiety from being unemployed and broke. The addict begins daydreaming and creates a fantasy of being a great doctor. The addict's obsession to be rescued and powerful triggers the union of the two codependent roles that create the addiction pathway and addict's loop. The addict creates images and stories of heroism. The addict might imagine grabbing the defibrillator paddles from a nurse and bringing a patient back to life (The doctor is symbolic of the controller rescuing the patient, which represents the broken and needy dependent.) The heroic "high" fantasy continues and the addict creates a beautiful house the doctor lives in and expensive sport cars the doctor owns and drives.

When the addict's loop runs out of obsessive fuel, the addict's heroic story fades. The addict comes down from his daydream and biochemical high and returns to the kitchen and discovers most of the dishes are washed, even though he doesn't remember much of his dishwashing experience. The addict begins experiencing uncomfortable waves of anxiety and depression. In the addict's loop, there is always a price to pay for experiencing the euphoric high/fix. To avoid the right side of the loop's *betrayal, rejection and abandonment,* the addict might return to his imaginary doctor's life or begin substance use to escape his now surfacing depression, powerlessness and less than default setting.

Over time, the addict's euphoric high/fix weakens and becomes dominated by his conscious and unconscious pain load. During the progression, the addict desperately attempts to escape and numb the rising pain load with substance and behavioral fixes. *The addict creates a self-drowning effect; the more he uses and fixes, the more unconscious pain load is recreated which attempts to surface into consciousness.* This unconscious process creates a building and breaking of the dam effect. The addict soon becomes defeated from his inability to control his unidentifiable surfacing pain load. It's as if an invisible wall of pain is moving toward the addict and he continues to "fix," believing his self-rescue mission and "high" will solve the problem and completely remove the approaching anxiety and pain. The rising and unidentifiable pain load finally creates a tidal wave effect that completely drowns and overpowers the addict. The addict's shame and loss of control leads to depression and isolation. To ask an addict to use willpower to control his addiction would be like asking someone to control their nocturnal dreams. In the later stages, the addict's conscious and unconscious pain load finally trumps the euphoric high/fix and walks the addict toward insanity and death, unless the addict awakens from the two progressive loops.

Chapter 5

The Echo Shaming And Abandonment Of The Codependent And Addict's Core Identity

Echo Shaming *is the unconscious learned behavior of a dependent and controller receiving critical and shaming abuse and making it his own pain, inner voice and experience. Echo shaming gravitates the child into the inherited and programmed codependent role(s).*

Each time the codependent *splits* from his core identity, it creates the cruel illusion that the child is leaving something bad and arriving into something where he will be received and loved. The dependent child's unconscious transformation into the dependent role becomes, *"I will abandon myself, people please and become what you want, so I am visible and loved."* The controller child's transformation becomes, *"I will abandon myself and rescue and enable you, so I am visible and loved."* The echo shaming from the codependent and addict's authentic self is a painful, traumatic and lonely journey. Every codependent and addict has his own story and journey of *echo shaming* out of his root honesty and authentic self. During a workshop a man named David shared his story...

I remember being a dependent to my mother's controller role. I was echo shamed out of my root honesty by my mother. Her harsh words would spin in my head and criticize my thinking, feelings and behavior. I would not repeat my mother's shaming words when they were spoken, but later, if I were building a small model airplane and accidentally broke the plastic landing wheel, I would echo shame my mother's words "you can't do anything right." My echo shaming pattern repeated itself whenever I "screwed up" or thought I screwed up and I soon learned to become negative, critical and judgmental toward myself and my world. My mother passed her shaming, critical voice to me, and it became my new inner voice condemning my thoughts and feelings.

During my conditioning, the process of echo shaming became self-fulfilling. If my mother wasn't around to criticize and shame me, I would sabotage myself and unconsciously create the circumstances to fail and condemn myself. My unconscious programming created a bizarre "failure fix," whenever life was good and going my way. I would project my "failure fix" onto my life and become forgetful or clumsy and accidentally break something or be neglectful. My mother would then criticize and lecture me for screwing up and I would stand trance-like and believed I deserved the verbal or physical abuse. Later in life, when I confronted my mother about her extremely controlling, dominating and critical behavior she seemed confused and didn't remember a lot of the circumstances.

An example of echo shaming for a child-controller would be a "dependent" family member unconsciously baiting, leaning on, manipulating and guilt tripping the child-controller to rescue and save him. Again, the controller is also driven by fear of abandonment, his internal message being, *"If I don't rescue and save the dependent, I will be abandoned and alone."* The child-controller is conditioned and learns to become enabling, critical, angry and a victim of the family dependent(s).

In the story above, David describes the dependent role creating a "failure fix." This is one of the most tragic, unconscious messages and programming embedded in the dependent role. For example, let's revisit the young baseball player. Remember when the dependent boy played his second game and walked six players? I purposely placed something in the story. During the second game, when the dependent boy walks six players and hits a grounder into center field, he runs around the bases and...do you remember what happens before he's tagged out? *He trips and falls.* I made the young dependent son *trip and fall* for a reason. This becomes the young dependent's "failure fix," an unconscious "SOS" to be rescued by the controller role. The night before the game the young boy lay in bed and feared disappointing his father. What the young boy fears and represses unfortunately happens. The dependent's unconscious message becomes, *"I cannot do this alone. I will screw it up and fail. I need my controller to rescue me."* Tragically, the young boy's repressed fears make him trip and fall, which triggers his father's frustration. The controller's fear becomes, *"He keeps screwing up and is not going to make it in life.* " What the father is actually reacting to is the dependent role's, "less than" programming and embedded "failure fix." The dependent might have great potential and succeed for a while but then "screws up" and returns to his "less than" default setting. The dependent's "less than" default setting, triggers the rescue mission for the controller to step in and save the dependent. Both codependent roles end up frustrated, angry, defeated and heart broken. The addict's internal and programmed "failure fix" becomes a powerful embedded trigger to recreate his own internal rescue mission.

Write below your own personal experience of being echo shamed.

Remember, echo shaming is when you started to self-condemn yourself and to believe the criticism and manipulation that made you enter into your codependent role(s).

For the one split codependent (dependent or controller), write any memory of being echo shamed out of your authentic self and into your controller <u>or</u> dependent role.

For the addict, write any memories of being echo shamed out of your authentic self and into the controller <u>and</u> dependent roles.

_____

_____

_____

_____

_____

_____

If you have the dependent role, how do you personally relate to the "failure fix?"

If you're an addict, give an example that does not include returning to your addiction. The "failure fix" pattern is getting ahead in your life and then "screwing up" and returning to your "less than" default setting. Becoming aware, understanding and counter-conditioning the "failure fix" pattern dismantles one of the most powerful triggers of addiction. *An example could be starting a business which at some point fails before opening its doors to the public. Identifying your "failure fix" pattern, you discover you sabotaged your business, fearing its success and/or failure. Another example could be a relationship where you constantly "screw up" and become shameful and "less than" and unconsciously set yourself up to be criticized, rescued and lectured by your controller. Because of your dependent role's "failure fix," you abandon the relationship and relapse.*

The Addict Rotates Between The Two False Worlds Of Controller And Dependent, Trying To Find His Way Home

I'd like to share an observation I had while sitting in an Al-Anon meeting. I had completed most of my addiction model and had one of those late-night "light bulb" moments. Looking around the room, I realized a large percentage of Al-Anon members are one-split controllers who gravitate to *rotators*, where the addict has a dominant dependent role. This is why I have rarely witnessed Al-Anon members dating and marrying each other. I believe if two controllers are in a relationship, they have done extensive 12-step and/or therapy to counter-condition their unconscious codependent behavior.

Addicts rotate and have both controller and dependent roles inherited and conditioned in their unconscious. This is why addicts attract, date and marry each other. An addict with a dominant controller role will gravitate to an addict with a dominant dependent role, and vice versa. I believe most addicts have completely echo shamed and abandoned their core identity, fully relying and rotating their two codependent roles. A high-functioning addict with a dominant controller role, who builds a career and works his way up the corporate ladder, can fuel his euphoric high/fix and illusion that his success "high" can heal his dependent role's "less than" default setting and the controller's feelings of powerlessness. When power and success are fleeting and don't "fix" the addict's "less than" default setting or feelings of powerlessness, the addict can sabotage his career and seek other substance or behavioral fixes, attempting to recreate his internal rescue mission.

The Codependent Relationship of Hank and Carla

Hank and Carla meet at a party, and they have an immediate attraction. They begin spending many days and nights with each other and are seen together most of the time. Their lovemaking is passionate, excessive and magical. When they're not together, they text each other and talk on the phone several times each day. Even though they experience a euphoric high in the relationship, they also experience continual waves of anxiety and fear. Hank fears he will be used and abandoned. Carla fears she will let Hank down, not be good enough and ultimately will be abandoned. For now, the euphoria in their relationship overpowers their fears and they enjoy each other and feel powerfully connected. Carla tells Hank she believes he's the "Knight in Shining Armor" she's been waiting for all her life and she fantasizes about having lots of children with him. Hank also feels Carla is the woman he's been searching for and he's finally found his soul mate.

Four weeks into their relationship, Carla moves in with Hank. The next day, Hank tells Carla he wants to get married in one year, have three children in five years and build a house in the suburbs on land his parents own. Hank wants Carla to live on the land with him in a large trailer and help build their first house together. Carla tells Hank it sounds good, but right now she needs to find a job because she's getting low on finances and several bills are overdue. Hank gives Carla money to pay her bills and shows her employment opportunities on the internet. Carla takes notes and applies for one of the jobs. The company calls Carla for an interview, but she doesn't show up and doesn't call to reschedule, which seems to happen more than once. Hank becomes upset and lectures Carla about being unprofessional and tells her that she needs to get her life together. He becomes concerned about her irresponsible behavior and wonders what kind of mother she will make. Carla feels terrible, but always seems to have an excuse that makes the other person at fault.

During their relationship Carla complains about her life, leans on Hank, and needs him to resolve most of her problems. Hank feels loved and needed giving Carla advice, but she rarely follows through with it. This causes Hank to become extremely frustrated and he starts raising his voice at Carla. During the relationship Carla loses control of her sweet tooth and indulges in her late night snacks and gains weight. She also becomes more and more distant and emotionally unavailable. Carla begins spending more time with her girlfriends and chatting on the phone. Hank progressively spends long hours on the internet.

One day Hank sets up a time for Carla to meet him at his parents' land, where Hank wants to build their future house together. Carla doesn't show up and doesn't call. Later, Hank confronts Carla and she has another excuse. Hank gets very angry and continues to lecture her on being irresponsible and selfish. The next week, Carla finds part time work, but it's not enough to cover her expenses. Hank gives her more money and helps her find a job at a friend's company. Carla begins working there, but constantly shows up late and doesn't like the job. She quits after two weeks. Hank lectures Carla for being ungrateful, irresponsible and lazy. Carla breaks down and tells Hank the relationship has too much pressure and she's tired of him always trying to control her. Hank tells Carla he's done and wants her to move out.

Carla starts packing her bags, but Hank changes his mind and begs her to stay. They make up and promise each other that they'll make adjustments in the relationship. Hank will stop lecturing Carla, and Carla will get a job and stop leaning on Hank for financial support. Hank and Carla are content, passionate and happy for a while, but the same destructive pattern begins to repeat itself. Hank continues to control, lecture and rescue Carla's broken life and Carla resents Hank's "know-it-all" lectures and continues being irresponsible and distant. Their sex life begins to fade.

One day Hank notices Carla slurring her words and asks if she's been taking drugs. Carla tells Hank she doesn't take drugs and yells at him for micromanaging her life again. While Carla's away, Hank goes through her belongings and finds an empty bottle of Vicodin. Later, he confronts Carla with the empty Vicodin bottle, and Carla rages at Hank for going through her things, packs her bags and leaves. Hank stops Carla and grabs her by the neck. Carla screams and hits Hank, runs to her car and drives away. Hank calls Carla and apologizes on her phone message, but Carla doesn't return any of his calls. Hank feels terrible and continues calling her and several of her friends. One of Carla's friends thinks she might be at her ex-boyfriend's house. Hank arrives and sees Carla with her ex-boyfriend. Carla confesses to Hank and tells him she's been taking Vicodin for several weeks. She tells Hank it helps her to relax and feel like she's not under his microscope all the time. Carla wants out of the relationship. She feels she can't do anything right around Hank and is tired of him controlling her life. Hank leaves but calls Carla every day, leaving angry messages about Carla using him and saying that he wants all of his money back. Hank also threatens to beat up Carla's ex-boyfriend. Hank arrives home one day and finds all of Carla's belongings gone. She's left a note saying *"I don't love you anymore, stay out of my life or I'll get a restraining order."* Hank is devastated and heartbroken, and becomes extremely angry and depressed, but also feels oddly relieved. Hank realizes that Carla was draining, entitled, spoiled and lazy.

Three months later Hank sees Carla at a local grocery store. Carla has moved into a girlfriend's house and is not seeing her ex-boyfriend. Three weeks later, Carla is living with Hank again. Their passion and euphoric connection is powerful but brief. Hank and Carla's relationship progresses but this time becomes extremely abusive. During one of their many fights, Hank gives Carla a black eye. Carla gets a restraining order against Hank and soon enters treatment for her opiate and food addiction. Hank's obsessive use of the internet becomes controllable. Hank blames Carla's irresponsible behavior and drug addiction for all his problems during the relationship. Carla believes she was a victim of Hank's control, rage and abuse.

Questions:

1) In the relationship of Hank and Carla, who was the "controller" and who is the "rotator?"
Hank is the controller and Carla is an addict "rotator" with a dominant dependent role and back seat controller.

2) What were the warning signs of their codependence?
Accelerated relationship, obsessive calling and contacting each other several times a day, moving in together in a short amount of time. Obsessive fear of being together and apart. Hank fears being used and abandoned and Carla fears not being good enough and ultimately being abandoned. Their fears become a fulfilling

prophesy of the addict's loop and its unconscious mechanics.

3) What codependent patterns occurred in the relationship?
Hank was controlling and tried to rescue and save Carla. He was blinded to Carla's shortcomings, and did not see how irresponsible and dishonest she was. When Carla didn't follow his directions, he became angry, intolerant and abusive. Carla was dishonest and "people pleased," leaned on Hank and wanted him to fix her problems, but then resented him when he tried. Carla continued to reject Hank's control and abandoned him in the relationship.

4) Who experienced the "Failure Fix?"
Carla's dependent role continually recreates and experiences the "failure fix." For example, Carla starts a job and continually shows up late. Because of Carla's dependent role and embedded "failure fix," Carla quits her job or gets fired, which triggers her "less than" default setting to be rescued by her controller.

5) What could Hank have done differently to stop his codependence in the relationship?
If Hank counter-conditioned his controller role, he would have learned to slow down the relationship and allowed Carla to be responsible for her own choices and broken life. Hank would have learned to be supportive, but not enable Carla by paying her bills and finding her work. Hank would have stopped trying to control and save Carla, thereby risking possible abandonment. Hank's controller programming creates the destructive and fearful message, "If I don't control and rescue Carla, she'll abandoned me." By counter-conditioning this unconscious message, Hank surrenders his controller role and learns to negotiate and be loved as an equal in the relationship.

6) What could Carla have done differently to stop her codependence in the relationship?
If Carla counter-conditioned her dependent role, she would have learned to move more slowly in the relationship and be honest about her life instead of being dishonest and needy with Hank. Carla would have learned to be self-supporting in the relationship and not accept Hank's money. Also, Carla's dependent role would

have learned to "step up" and set boundaries with Hank's controlling behavior. For example, Carla could confront Hank and say, "I love you but please stop trying to control and rescue me, I need to figure this out by myself."

7) How does the "addict's loop" apply to their story?
On the left "attraction" side of the loop (the connection, love bond and "euphoric high/fix"), Hank and Carla are obsessively attracted and enmeshed, and the relationship is accelerated and magical. They both share the experience of finding their soulmates and dream of a future and family together. The beginning of their relationship represents the euphoric high/fix, where all shortcomings and potential abuse are blocked by the denial side of the addict's loop. Because of the deceptive addict's loop, Hank and Carla believe their euphoric high will last forever.

As the relationship enters and reveals the right, "denial side" of the loop (the betrayal, rejection, abandonment and fear of non-existence), Carla is revealed to be irresponsible and leans on Hank to fix her broken life. Hank is revealed to be extremely controlling and treats Carla like a child. As the relationship progresses, Hank's frustration, temper and anger start to surface and Carla shuts down and isolates, rejecting Hank's control, abuse and domination.

When the relationship completely transitions into the right side of the addict's loop, it triggers Carla's internal rescue mission. Carla's internal message becomes, "You're not fixing me and creating our codependent high, so I must create it in myself." Both Hank and Carla start self-medicating their surfacing emotional pain and fears of rejection and abandonment. Hank obsessively uses the internet, and Carla overeats and uses drugs. When Carla abandons Hank, he becomes physically violent. Hank's violence represents his rage from years of circling the addict's loop and repressing his betrayal, rejection and abandonment. Three weeks later, they start the relationship again. The relationship progresses and is, once again, blinded by the euphoric high/fix and in complete denial of the right side of the addict's loop betrayal, rejection and abandonment.

8) Which codependent experiences substance abuse?

Hank is a one-split controller who does not rotate and is not an addict like Carla. What Hank can experience is substance abuse, or the illusion of addiction (his progressive internet use), that will become manageable once the relationship ends or he learns to set healthy boundaries.

Counter-conditioning codependence does not take the passion out of relationships. It restores the passion and keeps it active and alive. Codependence is not our authentic and true experience of love. Codependence will seduce and create a powerful euphoric passion and connection and then completely destroy the passion and the relationship and discard the personality. Codependence makes the codependent and addict feel broken, worthless, unlovable and alone. Many codependents, tragically, give up on love and isolate their lives away.

Chapter 6

The Origins Of Codependence And Addiction

The Original Unconscious Pain Load - The inherited controller and dependent roles, their destructive programming and pain load that are passed through generations. For example, *five generations of fathers have abused their sons and daughters. Each time the abuse is repressed because the child blocks it in the addict's loop and can only experience the euphoric connection to feel safe and loved. The multi-generational repressed abuse is passed and recreated in each generation. The multi-generational abuse becomes the "original unconscious pain load" that is handed down to each generation.*

Man-Made Hell - Man's real and imagined lies, fears, torture, ghost stories, rituals, superstitions, barbaric practices, abuse, rage, emotional pain, shame, guilt ... are repressed and stored in the unconscious. The collective, repressed chaos and pain of these emotions, visuals and experiences create the mythological monsters, demons, illnesses and disorders that are recreated in ourselves and each generation and projected onto our exterior world.

I believe codependence and addiction have been around for thousands of years. Within codependence travels the *original unconscious pain load,* which arrives and patiently waits for each codependent and addict's birth and arrival. Codependents can either inherit a one-split role (the controller or dependent) or both roles and become addict-rotators. The unconscious codependent and addict's programmed behavior is set before birth and learned before leaving home. Under the influence of the two codependent roles, families and role models will unconsciously determine how much abuse, trauma, emotional pain and rage will pass to the next generation. Many families will pass the *original unconscious pain load* with a vengeance, while others will deflect and dissipate its ageless fear, abuse, pain and destructive behavior.

Pain Load Peak

If the *original unconscious pain load* is not tempered with positive role models, therapy and/or spirituality, it can surface and *pain load peak* and completely destroy the codependent, his relationships and surrounding innocents. We witness this in our society and media every day. Codependents who are held hostage during childhood years in the original unconscious pain load can be stripped of all compassion and become mechanized objects of destruction.

The *original unconscious pain load* has traveled through multiple generations and has been given the name of evil, Satan and the devil. Many of society's random murders are marked by violent and twisted ego inflation and the unconscious pain load peak of abuse and destruction, followed by the aggressor's self-destruction which symbolically sends the surfaced pain load back into the unconscious world.

During his pain load peak, the perpetrator takes on a possessed behavior creating a semi "blackout" effect during his murderous spree. If the perpetrators do not sacrifice themselves after their pain load peak, they can return empty, confused and devastated. Also, there are those who never return from their unconscious pain load and have been conditioned and exist in a human shell with no remorse, compassion or empathy for their destructive behavior. These codependents and addicts become the contemporary analogy of the "walking dead," completely consumed and manipulated by the original unconscious pain load.

It is my hope that someday there will be research and several tests that can measure and evaluate a child's original and conditioned unconscious pain load, in order to identify and counter-condition any potential destructive behavior passed down through the generations.

The Origins Of Codependence And Addiction

Ancient man feared the dark and worshiped the sun. The darkness of night affected basic survival. Primitive man could not see during the night and was vulnerable to nocturnal beasts. Darkness brought cold and created insecurity and fears of the unknown. The sun brought relief, warmth and visibility. The sun warmed the earth, brought light for hunting and growing crops and created security for survival. It's easy to understand why primitive and civilized man worshiped the sun and feared the darkness of night. The sun became man's "higher power", and great meaning and celebration were directed toward its source. Even though darkness appeared, man learned the sun would reappear and once again bring warmth and security. When fire was created, its warmth and light were also worshiped. Fire brought visibility to darkness and soothed the nocturnal fears. Man feared but respected darkness and became dependent on the sun and fire to survive. Man learned to respect and honor his fears and worship the powerful forces of nature. This simple relationship created human dependency and salvation with a "higher power" that did not manipulate and strip man of his dignity, skills and abilities. The sun and fire did not make man weaker; it helped man to become stronger, evolve and survive.

It Was Man's Jealousy Of The Gods...

I believe the beginning relationship patterns of codependence and addiction were created and conditioned when man became a powerful "controller" or "false god" over another man and population. To keep his power intact, the powerful controller needed another human to worship him and be dependent, subservient and needy. Survival of the fittest challenged the powerful controller who did not want to share or surrender his power and control. If the dependent challenged, threatened or did not obey the controller, he would most likely die a horrible death.

The sun never threatened man or said, *"If you do not worship me, I will abandon you and you'll die in the cold of night."* Fire never told man, *"If you do not obey me, you'll burn on a wooden stake."* I believe this shift from a true higher power that helped man evolve and survive to a controller-false god that kept man fearful, needy and subservient created the relationship patterns of codependence and addiction.

I do not believe nature is evil. Nature is in forward motion, evolving its brilliant, calculated chaos into a new order. Unfortunately, man can sometimes become a victim and be caught in the crosshairs of nature's forces. It is a fact that nature's power and destructive forces have temporarily devastated mankind throughout our history and evolution. I do not believe it was or will ever be personal. I do not believe tornadoes dislike people in the Midwest and continue to destroy their lives. I believe it was man's interpretation of nature's forces that created our deep fears and unconscious caverns in repressed man-made hell. Nature's darkness hid hungry beasts and cold, empty shadows that man learned to understand, adapt to and survive. Man's manipulation, interpretation and imagination of nature spun terrifying stories and created horrific rituals, monsters, superstitions and barbaric acts of torture. This included man's condemnation and interpretation of man's own nature.

The controller's arrogance and self-righteousness created its own rule book on how humanity should live, behave and die. Instead of man finding harmony with a true higher power, he was labeled and put into a box filled with fears, rules and orders, so he could control his own unpredictable and unique nature. These new fears and behaviors unconsciously conditioned dependent man to live in greater fear and to worship the controller in order to feel safe and survive. These new fears, rituals, oppression and superstitions created deep, repressed, unconscious caverns that harbored the horrific images and barbaric practices that made the journey into salvation more extreme, dramatic and euphoric.

The images etched into our deep unconscious of angry gods, ghost stories and wicked monsters in repressed man-made hell created the rule book for the dependent and controller relationship, which teaches that if you do not love and honor the powerful controller, you will live in fear and be abandoned and die a horrible death. If you follow the rules, the controller will save you and create a union of euphoria and salvation. If you continue to obey the rules, the powerful, controller will take care of you and spare you from man-made hell, which was created to keep you fearful, needy and broken. These same rules tested the powerful controller's vulnerability. The powerful controller needed to feel loved, worshipped and honored. Without praise and worship, the controller is like an actor on stage without an audience. Without followers and dependents, the powerful controller becomes abandoned, insecure and mortal. To keep his position of power, the controller rescued the dependent in man-made hell to feel powerful, immortal and worshipped.

To understand the origins of the controller and dependent role, one has to wrap one's head around the concept that these two roles were created in the unconscious and have lived there ever since. In the story below, I will explain how I believe the two codependent roles originated in the unconscious.

The Dependent And The Conjured Controller

There is a seven-year-old boy who lives in a small, rural town. Next door to the young boy is a beautiful, dense forest. The young boy loves to ride his bike and play in the forest, which is filled with innocent creatures that run and hide when children are nearby. One day the young boy goes camping with his neighbor, who brings his teenage son. For many years there has been a myth of a shadow creature that lives in the forest. The story is told that, during the darkness of night, the creature steps out of the shadow and kills little children, eats their hearts, and disappears back into the forest. The young boy has never heard the story.

That night around the campfire, the teenager, who's not afraid of the myth, tells the story of the shadow creature, which deeply frightens the young boy. The boy becomes so terrified that he refuses to enter the forest, even during the day. While at school, the young boy hears more stories about the shadow creature. He learns that the shadow creature has large black eyes and a snake's tongue and sometimes kidnaps children from their beds and drags them off into the dark forest. At night, the young boy is so frightened that he can't sleep and is paralyzed with fear, imagining the shadow creature entering his room and eating his heart. The young boy's fears are so overwhelming that he blocks them out and represses them in order to cope and survive. The more he fears the shadow creature, the more he represses his thoughts and feelings. The more he represses his thoughts and fears, the deeper man-made hell is created in his unconscious. I have named the child's repressed fears "man-made hell" to represent the multi-generational significance of the shadow creature myth. The teenage boy and school friends did not create the myth. The story was created by man and passed down through the generations, where it was feared and repressed in the unconscious and became a part of the *original unconscious pain load.*

One day, the image of a superhero appears in the young boy's consciousness. The boy begins to fantasize about the superhero's abilities and how the superhero can easily destroy the shadow creature. The super hero is the powerful, rescuing, *controller role.* The boy gives the heroic controller role a name and mimics the controller's powers. His new imaginary, heroic controller makes the young boy feel protected, rescued and safe. Whenever the child is fearful, he visualizes the imagined heroic controller and himself destroying the forest shadow creature. The boy's imaginary hero controller is also from the unconscious and creates the illusion of escaping the child's deep fears (the shadow monster).

Because the two roles, the dependent and controller, were created in the unconscious, they can only create a temporary illusion of escape into euphoric salvation. The boy then reawakens back in his fears and abandonment. The reawakening and realization of being abandoned in man-made hell with the images of the shadow creature creates more fear and obsession to escape, and so the boy, once again, conjures his heroic controller to rescue him and lift him above his fears into a union of euphoric salvation. One day at school, the young boy makes friends with an older boy who fits the heroic, controller role. The young boy's new friend does not fear the shadow creature and they both fantasize about destroying it together.

The child's deep repressed fears of the shadow monster creates an imbalance in the young boy's psychology. The imbalance triggers a defense mechanism which creates a counter image of the heroic controller. The young child did not analyze himself and discover that his deep fears needed a hero and leader to rescue him. The child's deep fears and psychological imbalance create the heroic controller, which creates the temporary illusion of rescuing the fearful, dependent boy into euphoric salvation. When the boy unconsciously created or "conjured" his internal, heroic controller role, it simultaneously projected the controller role into the boy's exterior world to be fulfilled. The young boy then gravitates to his new friend, who had inherited and unconsciously learned the rescuing and powerful controller role.

And so … man's relationship with a true higher power who self-actualized him and his core abilities and made him stronger was hijacked by new and terrifying man-made fears, superstitions and barbaric rituals. To cope and survive, man repressed his fears, which created the helpless dependent in man-made hell. From the imbalance of the repressed and fearful dependent, a psychological defense mechanism triggers and creates a counter image of a heroic controller (false god) to save and rescue the helpless dependent. Because both roles are created in the unconscious, they can never leave. Both roles are separated and create a temporary euphoric union and illusion of escape, only to reawaken in the unconscious to re-experience their separation, powerlessness, shame, fear and pain and begin the process all over again. I believe over thousands of years this unconscious pattern created the addict's loop, which then created the biochemical loop.

Chapter 7

The Spiritual Transformation When Chaos Peaks

The Story Of The Eskimo

Two men are sitting in a diner in Alaska. One ask the other, "Do you believe in God?" The man replies, "Nope." The other man asks, "Why?" The man replies, "Two weeks ago I was out in the wilderness and it started snowing and I lost my direction. It kept snowing and got colder and my body started to freeze and get numb all over, so I got on my knees and prayed to God to save me, help me find my way back home ... nothing happened ... because God doesn't exist. Then I lost consciousness." The other man asks, "How did you get here?" The man replies, "Oh, some Eskimo came along and carried me into town."

Darwin's Theory, "Survival Of The Fittest"

The strong survive and carry their seeds forward to produce a stronger offspring. In Darwin's theory, the Eskimo should not have risked his own life to save the unconscious, freezing man. Why did the Eskimo carry the complete stranger into town? The stranger was not related to the Eskimo or his culture, so why did the Eskimo go out of his way to save the man?

Air Florida Flight 90

In Washington, D.C. on January 13, 1982, during an extraordinary period of freezing weather, Air Florida Flight 90 took off from nearby Washington National Airport, failed to gain altitude, and crashed into the 14th Street Bridge, where it hit six cars and a truck on the bridge, killing four motorists. After the devastating crash on the bridge, the plane then continued forward and plunged into the freezing Potomac River where only the tail section, which had broken off, remained afloat. Only six of the airliner's 79 occupants survived the initial crash and were able to escape the sinking plane in the middle of the ice-choked river.

Arland Dean Williams Jr., a banker from Atlanta, was one of the six survivors clinging to the twisted wreckage bobbing in the icy Potomac when the helicopter arrived twenty minutes after the crash. To the copter's two-man crew, Arland seemed the most alert. Life vests were dropped, then a flotation ball. Arland Williams Jr. passed the life vests and floatation ball, one by one, to the other five passengers. On two occasions, the crew recalled, he handed away a lifeline from the helicopter that could have dragged him to safety. The helicopter crew, which rescued five people, lifted a woman to the riverbank, then dragged three more persons across the ice to the shore. A woman who was trying to swim away from the sinking wreckage was too weak to grab the line again and started to drown in the icy water when a bystander, government office assistant *Lenny Skutnik,* stripped off his coat and boots, and in short sleeves dived into the icy water and swam out and saved her. The helicopter pilot, Donald W. Usher, returned to the plane crash and Arland Dean Williams Jr., the man who helped save the only five survivors, was gone.

What happened to Arland Dean Williams Jr? Why did he hand the life jackets, lifeline and floatation ball to his fellow passengers after waiting in the freezing water for 20 minutes? Survival of the fittest would dictate that Arland should grab the lifeline and save himself. Why did Lenny Skutnik take off his warm clothes, risk his life and dive into the icy waters to save the female passenger? What possible transformation happened to Arland Dean Williams and Lenny Skutnik at the crash site?

Philippine Man Saves Dozens Of People From Floods

An 18-year-old construction worker, *Muelmar Magallanes*, was at home on Saturday with his family when tropical storm Ketsana unleashed the heaviest rains in more than 40 years on the Philippine capital and surrounding areas. Magallanes and his father quickly decided to evacuate their family once they realized the river, 800 meters away, had burst its banks. With the help of an older brother, Magallanes tied a rope around his waist and attached it one-by-one to his three younger siblings, whom he took to higher ground. He then came back for his parents. After helping his parents to higher ground, Magallanes, a strong swimmer, decided to go back for neighbors trapped on their rooftops. He ended up making many trips and eventually saved more than 30 people from drowning. Tired and shivering, Magallanes was back on higher ground with his family when he heard Ms. Penalosa screaming as she and her baby were being swept away on a wooden box they were using in an attempt to cross the swift currents.

Magallanes dived back in after the mother and daughter, who were already a few meters away and bobbing precariously among the debris floating on the brown water. "I didn't know the current was so strong. In an instant, I was under water. We were going to die," said Ms Penalosa, her eyes welling with tears and voice choking with emotion." Then this man came from nowhere and grabbed us. He took us to where the other neighbors were, and then he was gone," Ms Penalosa said. Ms Penalosa and other witnesses said that an exhausted Magallanes was simply washed away amid the torrent of water. Neighbors found his body on Sunday, along with 28 others who perished amid Manila's epic flooding.

LOGAN, Utah -- In comic books, superheroes are often depicted as lone wolves. But in a horrifying car-motorcycle crash in Logan, Utah, on a Monday, heroes came in bunches. Looking like a cross-section of America, hard-hat construction workers, a businessman, a woman in skirt and sandals and a man dressed for leisure in t-shirt and shorts suddenly appeared to free 21-year-old Brandon Wright as he lay trapped beneath a burning BMW on a city street. Logan's assistant chief of police, Jeff Curtis, says the department is now trying to find out just who these rescuers were, and told NBC News their efforts, at their own considerable peril, saved Wright's life. "They're rescuers; they did a great job of getting him the help that he needed," Curtis said. "I'm impressed they would risk their own safety to lift the car up and get the individual out from underneath it." At first, a construction worker appeared, trying to lift the rear end of the BMW on his own. Within seconds, he's joined by four others, who try in vain to lift the two-ton car. Suddenly, other on-the-spot rescuers enter the picture, and with a dozen folks pitching in, they manage to raise the burning car while a construction worker drags Wright's motionless body out from under the wreckage. In a T.V. interview, Wright thanked the anonymous group from his hospital bed a few days later.

Spiritual Brownouts

There are thousands of these stories happening every day that we never hear about. An anonymous stranger risks his life to save another human being and then moves on as if nothing happened. These *"spiritual brownouts"* are what I believe to be one of the most powerful signs of and connection with a higher power.

I'd like to share a personal story that happened to me a few months ago. At 1:30 A.M. my phone rang with my mother's name on the caller ID (not a good time to get a call from mom). A woman on the phone informed me that my mother had fallen asleep at the wheel, totaled her car and three parked cars. The woman said my mother was very shaken but doing okay. When my son and I arrived at the accident site, there were crushed auto parts, glass and metal everywhere. The woman who contacted me had brought my mother a chair and had organized all her paperwork for the police. She was now standing behind my mother, comforting her. The woman asked me if she could help in any other way, and I let her know I could manage and that her help was greatly appreciated. My son guided my mother to my car while I spoke with the police, who told me they had all the information from the stranger who had come to my mother's aid. I turned to wave and thank the woman one more time, but she was gone.

Chaos And A New Order

Historically, when a civilization went into darkness and the scales were tipped into the imbalance of chaos, misery, despair and destruction, did an "enlightened" prophet suddenly appear and guide the civilization back into its spiritual center, through sacrifice, rebirth and reconstruction?

When a star's energy collapses and explodes into a Super Nova, does the Super Nova's chaos become a new order through sacrifice, rebirth and reconstruction? The sun collapses, dies and explodes, sending billions of incubated subatomic particles into the universe to recreate new life and a new order.

I would like you to think about your own emotional, mental chaos with codependence and addiction. When you were lost in the deep despair of chaos and destruction, did someone show up in your life with loving, unselfish eyes, watching and caring about you? Who was it? A parent, a friend, a cousin, brother or sister, a neighbor, a stranger?

Write any memories of when you were in great emotional pain and despair and someone showed up for you, guided you and expected nothing.

_____

_____

_____

_____

_____

_____

_____

Addiction And The Spiritual Awakening And Experience

A man slowly walks the perimeter of his darkened basement. He has painted the small windows black and the floor is covered with leaking water and trash from his self-confinement. No substance or behavioral fix can save him. The man's new obsession is suicide, before his undefinable waves of pain swallow him whole and deliver him into the undertow of his insanity.

From the far corner of the basement, a small hole suddenly appears in the ceiling, shooting a ray of bright light into the man's darkened world. Curious, the man uses a stick and pokes at the small hole, which suddenly begins to widen with a domino effect, splintering the ceiling into a thousand pieces. In a matter of seconds, the entire basement and cinder block walls collapse and completely cover the man with debris. The defeated man lays under the thick debris and believes this is the end. He's ready to die. Suddenly, he experiences a shift from deep inside. The man's "self-talk" whispers the simple words, "Save yourself." The man struggles, pushes off the debris, and slowly crawls out of his collapsed basement onto his front yard. He lies in his front yard and looks up at the night sky trying to catch his breath. Tears roll down his cheeks and he feels a raw sense of himself connected to the stars and universe above. The man turns to his side and sees his entire house has collapsed and is completely destroyed. It is at this moment that he realizes he must salvage what he can and build a new house.

Neighbors come to his aid and offer the man lodging while he builds his new house. They also offer their services and skills and bring tools and years of experience. Together, they work and completely build a new house from the foundation up. When they are finished, the man opens his doors to his new friends and feels a deep connection to himself, his neighbors and life. This man has had a spiritual awakening and spiritual experience. The man's pain load peak triggers his spiritual awakening (the hole and light breaking into his darkness), which triggers his crumbling house of addiction. The man's spiritual awakening and experience transforms his chaos into salvation, rebirth and reconstruction, into a new order.

Imagine the crumbling house, airplane crash, the burning car, the chaos of addiction and codependence inside your mind. Was there a sign, an abstract visual, an out-of-body experience, your commanding or subtle voice, a dream, a bright light? Did anything appear when you reached the bottom of your own personal chaos? What happened at that moment of clarity, the jumping off point when you were standing on your emotional cliff, possibly contemplating suicide, completely giving up, surrendered? What changed? What became clear? What spiritual awakening entered into your being when your own personal chaos peaked and the message of salvation, rebirth and reconstruction appeared?

Write your own experience of a spiritual awakening.

_____

_____

_____

_____

_____

_____

_____

_____

_____

_____

_____

_____

_____

_____

Chapter 8

The Damaging Effects Of Codependence In 12-Step Programs

I believe the most difficult transition in recovery is breaking free, or bottoming out, from the addict's unconscious controller and dependent roles. Dr. Carl Jung said that an alcoholic must have a spiritual experience, one which involves a huge emotional upheaval and replacement of ideas, emotions and attitudes. I also believe the spiritual experience, or awakening, is the deep shift from the two inherited and destructive codependent roles, back into one's buried core identity and root honesty that was echo shamed and abandoned during childhood years.

The two codependent roles create an unconscious dictatorship where the controller becomes the dependent's false god. The codependent dictatorship is a closed system and has no spiritual connection because the dependent is programmed to make the controller its higher power. Within the covert dictatorship, the controller cannot allow the dependent to grow, self-actualize and become equal or more powerful. The dependent is programmed to stay broken, needy and entitled. The relationship is rigid, with a thick rulebook that creates dishonest performances and the illusion of feeling rescued, secure, loved and connected at the euphoric high/fix. The addict's codependent roles and biochemical *fixes* sooner or later progress and then self-destruct, leaving the addict devastated, abandoned, broken and helpless.

Breaking Down The 12-Steps And Unconscious Codependence

The first of the 12-steps identifies that the addict has lost complete control of his substance and/or behavioral fixes and his life has become unmanageable, rotating the unconscious roles of the controller and dependent.

Steps 2 and 3 set in motion the shift from unconscious codependence to a spiritual power, or "power greater than ourselves," that creates a new spiritual center of gravity in order for the addict's abandoned root honesty and core identity to be realigned and self-actualize. By creating a "power greater than ourselves," the addict dismantles the needy dependent and controller-false god and surrenders the obsessive and temporary gratification of the euphoric high/fix. Simply, the addict learns to stay out of the "land of the fix," where the dependent leans on and breaks the controller and the controller over-controls and suffocates the dependent.

Over time, the spiritual process creates new, healthy boundaries that do not trespass and destroy the addict's life and relationships. An analogy might be a plant that has lived in a garden infested with weeds. Over time, the weeds strangle and bend the plant completely over. One day, a gardener uproots the plant and replants it in a weed-free environment, with rich soil, the perfect amount of water and sunshine (this would be the plant's spiritual center of gravity). Even though the plant has been freed from the weed-infested garden, the plant still grows as if the weeds continue to strangle it. Over time, the plant's healthy environment, or spiritual center of gravity, frees the plant into its natural growth and abundance. The transformation also represents the addict's continual process of the 12-steps.

Once the addict creates a surrender point and higher power, for the two codependent roles to be "turned over to," the surrender point must be nurtured because the two inherited codependent roles will rebuild and gravitate the addict back into codependence and the addict's loop. This power struggle becomes the addict's "spiritual tug of war" between the addict's two unconscious codependent roles and the addict's awakened core identity and root honesty.

The middle steps 4 through 9 define and rebuild the addict's reclaimed core identity and personal boundaries ("I've hurt you, I make amends, you hurt me, I set boundaries"). The middle steps also process and help uncover the addict's overwhelming unconscious pain load that continues to be recreated in himself and surrounding relationships.

When the addict bottoms out, he comes crashing down into his echo shamed core identity, which is filled with layers of emotional pain, collected from years of circling the addict's loop. For example, imagine visiting the house you lived in as a child. The house is dilapidated, boarded up, trash everywhere, holes in the walls, mud and water on the floors. This is your core that you learned to *echo shame*, distrust, destroy, abandon and condemn. With the middle steps, the addict cleanses his contaminated core identity and reclaims and rebuilds his abandoned self.

Because unconscious codependence gravitates the addict back into dishonest codependent roles and recreates his unconscious pain load, steps 10 and 11 are maintenance steps for the addict to stay in his reclaimed clean and sober core identity. Through meditation, the addict nurtures his "spiritual center of gravity" and reclaimed core identity, which creates a new awareness and keeps healthy boundaries intact.

Step 12 creates a proactive service to others, with no strings attached, creating unconditional love within balanced boundaries that do not trespass or destroy the addict and his relationships. These new boundaries are practiced in all the addict's relationships with people, places and things. If correctly adapted and applied, the 12-steps can help counter condition the unconscious and destructive roles of codependence. Unfortunately, I believe codependence is more powerful and continues to destroy the addict and erode the 12-step process.

I believe unconscious codependence has created confusion, alienation and relapse in 12-step programs. Over my years of sobriety, I have personally witnessed the controller and dependent roles projected in many 12-step sponsor/sponsee relationships. Codependence conflicts and damages the 12-step goals of building a clean and sober core identity, creating healthy boundaries and having unconditional love and a spiritual connection with a higher power. When unconscious codependence infiltrates 12-step relationships, the newcomer steps into the familiar dependent role he has been trained to perform all his life. Because addicts rotate, the dependent sponsee learns to become the "controller-sponsor," and it is passed to the next group of members and accepted as the "norm." These codependent sponsor/sponsee relationships create an unconscious dictatorship that contradicts, damages and confuses the 12-step process.

There is no chapter in the Big Book of AA that describes "Sponsoring Members," but all the information needed is in the chapter entitled "Working With Others", which very carefully explains in detail how to keep healthy boundaries intact when working with actively-using or clean and sober members. Unfortunately, codependence is more powerful and gravitates the 12-step member back into his unconscious codependent roles and continues to recreate the destructive "controller/dependent" relationships. There are many members who have learned to counter-condition their unconscious codependent roles and sponsor with healthy boundaries.

Another codependence trap in 12-step programs is making the controller role a higher power. Again, the sober member gravitates to the dependent role and creates a higher power that is a "rescuer" of the sober member's life. The addict's controller-higher power is praised as long as it continues to show signs and satisfies the addict's needs. The relationship between the dependent and higher power mimics the same dependent-controller programming, "you help and save me and I'll worship you." This may work temporarily and intermittently until something bad happens to the sober member and he feels *betrayed, rejected and abandoned* by his controller-higher power or false god. The betrayal, rejection, abandonment and disillusionment can lead to relapse.

I also have witnessed several 12-step romantic relationships unconsciously abandon the program and gravitate back into their codependent roles. The addict's loop, sooner or later, rejects, abandons and destroys the relationship and the addict becomes devastated and relapses. I'm not blaming anyone. This is what unconscious codependence does. It will conflict and war with any spiritual growth and path.

Bottoming Out, Surrendering, Conditional and Unconditional Spirituality And Finding 12-Step Sponsors
Bottoming Out

The addict's loop has crashed and burned. The euphoric high/fix has been flatlined and the addict's conscious and unconscious pain load has flooded the addict's reality. The horror is one day realizing that all the drugs, alcohol, sex, food, gambling, etc, didn't work and the terrifying fear of being dropped off the cliff into the abyss of nonexistence has replaced them. At the same time, a feeling of great relief and freedom can begin to enter the addict's life. The dishonest roles of the controller and dependent have been arrested. The covert dictatorship has been dismantled and the false god of the controller has failed, as historically all false gods self-destruct. Respect and nurture your root honesty and core identity because they will be challenged. Unfortunately, the addict's loop will begin to rebuild itself and be calling you to join its destructive process all over again.

The Difference Between Unconditional Spirituality And Conditional Spirituality

The Big Book of Alcoholics Anonymous does not have "conditional spirituality." It does not state that if you do not work through the 12 steps, you will be banned from the 12-step program and burn in hell. The 12-step program uses lots of religious words. It calls its God a "*he* and *himself,*" but its spiritual definition and foundation is an *unconditional, loving God of service*. For example, the third step and second tradition.

Step 3 - Made a decision to turn our will and our lives over to the care of God, as we understood Him.

When I first read the third step I thought, "*Oh no, they're forcing me to believe in their God which is a Him?*" The words, *as we understood Him,* became confusing and contradictory from a program that supposedly allowed me to choose my own interpretation of a higher power. Reading step 3, I felt I was being forced back into a conditional religious format. After reading the second tradition, I understood the structure of the program and its spiritual foundation.

For our group purpose, there is but one ultimate authority -- a loving God as He may express Himself in our group conscience.

In the tradition, it states that a *loving God* is the foundation of the program. There are no religious conditions, but obviously, lots of religious words are used to describe an unconditional loving God. I was not used to religious words describing an unconditional loving God without "conditions." I believe there are sentences in the Big Book where a condition is expressed using the word "must," but the foundation of the Big Book is designed as a program of suggestion, example and attraction. Over my years of sobriety, I have observed that most of the 12-step conditions are created within the codependent sponsor/sponsee relationships and misguided interpretation of the 12-step program.

In the 12-step program, it became my free choice to choose either, the 12-step unconditional, loving God (*He, Him, Lord, God*, etc.), or choose my own higher power and plug it into the format. For example, if my own personal higher power were "the great spirit", my own third step would be, "*Made a decision to turn my will and my life over to the care of the great spirit.*" This would become my own personal version of the program's third step. My participation in the 12-step program and group would follow the third tradition, which states, "*A loving God as He may express Himself in our group conscience.*" In the final breakdown, I have exercised my free will and chosen my own higher power, "*the great spirit,*" and practice the program's second tradition of *an unconditional, loving God*, using patience, love and tolerance within the 12-step groups. I consider this a spiritual program that allows several definitions of a higher power within its own structure and format.

Finding 12-Step Sponsors

One of the most challenging tasks for the newcomer or any member is finding a sponsor. As I mentioned above, I believe codependence can and does rule a great percentage of the sponsor/sponsee relationships and greatly damages the 12-step process. Again, I'm not criticizing or blaming the members. This is what unconscious codependence does until it becomes part of the addict's conscious awareness.

My suggestion for the newcomer, or any member seeking a sponsor, is to collect several phone numbers from members willing to sponsor. The goal is to interview the potential sponsor and find out how much of their program is based on their codependence and how much is based on the Big Book and the 12 steps. My observation is that the controller role (false god) *rules, dictates, micro-manages, puts their sponsee on a restrictive leash, talks down to them and can be verbally abusive.* The dependent role is usually *indifferent, unavailable, nonconfrontational and irresponsible.* What the newcomer or member should evaluate is what percentage of the controller and dependent role does the potential sponsor exhibit and express during the interview and how much do they use the Big Book "suggestion" format?

I believe no one is completely codependent free, so it becomes about weighing the pros and cons of what members offer in their sponsorship. You may have to be in a sponsor/sponsee relationship for a few weeks before any unconscious codependence becomes apparent. My experience is that the best sponsor doesn't tell you what to do but shares his own experiences and gives suggestions. He also might nudge his sponsees into doing their step work but does not order them around and make demands (in other words, stays out of the controller role). The sponsee needs to become self-motivated (out of the dependent role) and step forward and show willingness to do the work.

Also, there are several non-spiritual, self-help support groups that incorporate behavioral therapies, positive reinforcement strategies and self management tools. I personally believe these self-help groups and programs (SMART Recovery, SOS, Rational Recovery) can be very positive if the addict, at the same time, counter-conditions his unconscious codependence.

Chapter 9

Introduction To The Nine-Step Process For Counter Conditioning Addiction And Codependence

The one-split codependent (controller or dependent) can begin to counter-condition his one codependent role through the nine-step process beginning in chapter 10. Answer the questions that are directed toward your one codependent role. Remember, the one split codependent may rotate a few of his surrounding relationships but that does not mean he's an addict. You need to inherit both the addict's loop and biochemical loop to create addiction.

You do not need a higher power or spiritual program to do the nine steps, but you can integrate your own spiritual beliefs and practices. It is important to understand that addiction is not your fault. It is not your parents' fault or the fault of any family members or role models. Yes, your home environment and surrounding relationships can and will condition or *charge* your codependence and addiction patterns, but most of the conditioning is unconscious, which means very few are aware of their deep, inherited codependent programming and behavior. Only when unconscious patterns become conscious can we then become responsible.

I have designed the nine steps to help counter condition the unconscious patterns of codependence and addiction. I believe these steps will be most effective after you completely detox from your destructive addiction *fixes*. I use the word *destructive* because I believe there's a big difference between a caffeine addiction and a cocaine addiction. Of course, if caffeine addiction has ruined your life, you can always add it to your list of "destructive fixes." It is my belief that the number one addiction of every addict is relationship addiction. After that, addicts stack and switch other substance and behavioral fixes on top of their unconscious codependence.

Remember, multi-generational codependent patterns are unconscious, which means you may not have any awareness of how the codependent patterns manipulate and control your addiction, relationships, behavior and life. Because these unconscious patterns may be new to your awareness, it's important that you take your time and move slowly through the nine-step process. Many of you will not want to stir up your codependent patterns because you're still unconsciously protecting them. That's normal. But just remember, they will not magically disappear and will continue to recreate your unconscious pain load.

The goal is to separate the codependent roles from yourself and develop compassion for those who are still unaware and suffer from their codependent roles and behavior ... this includes yourself. The nine-step process is not about your surrounding relationships making adjustments for you, but you setting boundaries and making adjustments for your surrounding relationships. Hopefully, the people who love you will respect your new boundaries and work with you, while others may move on and so be it. If you are new to sobriety, I recommend that you see a therapist or counselor along with your self-help and support groups. It is important to create a circle of support around you. This is also important when you work the nine-step process and apply yourself to the counter conditioning tools.

The Nine Steps

Step 1- Know the unconscious controller and dependent roles inherited and conditioned in most addicts.

Step 2 - Learn how and why the addict rotates the two codependent roles.

Step 3 - Understand the addict's loop and biochemical loop in the addict.

Step 4 - Identify your two unconscious codependent roles.

Step 5 - Discover your surrounding codependent relationships

and your rotation pattern.

Step 6 - Uncover your original unconscious pain load and inherited behavior in the two codependent roles.

Step 7 - Identify your personal unconscious pain load which continues to recreate itself.

Step 8 - Reclaim your core identity and learn to live in your proactive present.

Step 9 - Counter-condition the addict's loop by living in your proactive present and nurture abundance without addiction fixes.

Chapter 10

The Nine-Step Process

Step 1
Know the unconscious controller and dependent roles inherited and conditioned in most addicts.

The one split codependent should answer the questions directed toward his one codependent role.

I have placed the breakdown of the two codependent roles of the controller and dependent below. Highlight or underline the traits and behavior you personally relate to in the codependent role(s).

The Controller

The controller child ("child" includes teen years) grows up feeling insecure and disconnected from his family and role models. The controller child spends hours alone, thinking, *"if only I were smarter, taller, better looking or perfect they would love me."* The child begins personalizing the family conflicts and feels responsible for solving the family problems. To survive, the child unconsciously splits from his authentic self to become a controlling pretend-parent toward the family dependent(s). The codependent split from his authentic self creates obsessive compulsive thinking and behavior.

Being the controller gives the child the experience of feeling loved, powerful and needed. The child's efforts create the illusion of being a hero who must constantly rescue and enable the family dependent(s). The dependent role is programmed to be "temporarily saved" but then returns to being needy and broken, which makes the controller child feel like a failure and abandoned. The controller's obsession to save the entitled and broken dependent creates a destructive definition of love, *"I am loved, honored and praised because you need me to rescue and enable you."* The controller's definition of love is soon followed by rejection and abandonment. This becomes the revolving-door pattern of the child controller.

The Dependent

The *dependent* child ("child" includes teen years) also grows up feeling insecure and disconnected from his family and role models. The dependent child becomes a dishonest "people pleaser" to avoid confrontation, criticism and humiliation from the family controller(s). The dependent's inherited programming sends the crippling message, *"I am broken, unworthy and needy, and because of this feel great shame."* The dependent child attempts to escape his shame by being likeable, funny, charming, cool, smart and tough, and survives by not "stirring the pot." The dependent child feels entitled to being rescued from his broken life. He is "temporarily rescued" by the controller but then always returns to his "less than" default setting.

The dependent child's split from his root honesty and authentic self also creates obsessive-compulsive thinking and behavior. Out of loyalty, guilt and devotion, the dependent child continues to dishonestly "people please" so he won't feel disconnected and alone. The dependent child is forced to live in a dishonest world and learns to lie, manipulate and become *passive-aggressive* to get his needs met. The dependent's false definition of love becomes, *"I am loved because you rescue and enable me and I praise and honor you."* The dependent's definition of love is soon followed by rejection and abandonment. This becomes the revolving door pattern of the child dependent.

Step 2
Learn how and why the addict rotates the two codependent roles.

Most addicts inherit and rotate both *controller* and *dependent* roles, which are permanently conditioned in the addict's unconscious. The dependent role might be conditioned or *charged* first from a family member who is an unconscious controller. At some point the child/teen will rotate, and the controller role will be conditioned from a dependent family member and/or central role model. During dependent conditioning, the child/teen addict will unconsciously echo shame, condemn and abandon his core identity and become broken, needy and entitled toward the family controller or controller role model.

The child/teen addict then rotates and conditions or *"charges"* the controller role and once again abandons his root honesty, but this time to rescue and enable the family dependent(s). When both roles are *"charged,"* the child/teen addict will completely abandon his core identity and rotate the two codependent roles in his surrounding relationships. More specifically, the addict still uses his physical and cognitive abilities, but unconsciously condemns and abandons (echo shames) his emotional life and spiritual connection and survives in the two codependent roles.

Answer the question below

Most of my childhood was a fog bank, but I do remember one day thinking to myself, *"I don't care anymore, I give up. I'll do anything they want."* Do you remember when you gave up and just played the game and did what they wanted?

_____

_____

_____

_____

_____

_____

_____

_____

_____

_____

_____

_____

_____

_____

_____

_____

Step 3
Understanding the addict's loop and biochemical loop in the addict.

The one split codependent can skip these two paragraphs and go to the questions below.

The two magnetic codependent roles gravitate and attract, creating a biochemical high on the unconscious addict's loop. The left side of the addict's loop, _longing, connection, love bond_, peaks at the _euphoric high/fix_ and creates the illusion of being secure and whole while temporarily escaping the addict's _betrayal, rejection and abandonment_. The addict's biochemical loop also seeks the euphoric high/fix in order to avoid his withdrawal, detox and hangover. Both loops create a blinding and obsessive euphoric high/fix that blocks any repercussions or consequences when connecting with the euphoric high/fix.

When the addict's euphoric high/fix runs out of obsessive fuel (runs out of drugs, etc.), the right "denial" side of both loops, each time, is newly revealed. The addict goes into a free fall and suddenly awakens from the euphoric high/fix into the right side of *betrayal, rejection and abandonment*. The biochemical loop's euphoric high/fix transitions the addict into *withdrawal, craving, depression and hangover*. The addict's combination of the two loops, *betrayal, rejection, abandonment, withdrawal, detox and hangover,* create the addict's motivation and craving to seek their euphoric high/fix. Both loops create a progressive self-drowning effect. The more an addict *fixes*, the more unconscious pain and craving is triggered, which motivates his escape into the euphoric high/fix.

Questions for the one split codependent and addict.

How do you personally relate to the *euphoric high/fix?*

_____

_____

_____

How do the words on the right side of the addict's loop, *betrayal, rejection, abandonment and fear of non existence,* personally affect you? What feelings do they bring or stir up from your childhood and adult relationships?

_____

_____

_____

_____

_____

_____

_____

_____

_____

_____

Step 4
Identify your two unconscious codependent roles.

The one split codependent should answer the questions directed toward his one codependent role.

Your Dependent Role During Child/Teen Years.

1) Who were your controller(s) during child/teen conditioning years?

_____

_____

_____

_____

_____

_____

2) Do you remember becoming dishonest and "people pleasing" your controller(s)? Give example.

_____

_____

_____

_____

_____

_____

_____

_____

3) Do you remember trying to fit in and becoming accepted by your controller(s)? Give an example.

_____

_____

_____

_____

_____

_____

4) Did you get angry or abandon your controller if your controller(s) did not rescue and take care of you? Give an example.

_____

_____

_____

_____

_____

_____

5) For the addict: If you were a dependent first, when did you rotate into the controller role?

_____

_____

_____

_____

Your Controller Role During Child/Teen Years.

1) Who were your dependent(s) during child/teen conditioning years?

_____

2) How did it make you feel being a controller?

_____

_____

_____

_____

_____

_____

3) What did you believe would happen if you did not rescue your dependent(s)? Give an example.

_____

_____

_____

_____

_____

_____

_____

_____

_____

_____

_____

_____

4) Did you feel like a victim taking care of your dependents? Describe an experience.

_____

_____

_____

_____

_____

_____

_____

_____

5) What did you do if your dependent(s) did not follow your directions and advice? Give an example.

_____

_____

_____

_____

_____

_____

_____

_____

_____

6) For the addict: if you were a controller first, when did you rotate into the dependent role?

_____

_____

_____

_____

_____

Step 5
Discover your surrounding codependent relationships and your rotation pattern.

The one split codependent should answer the questions directed toward his one codependent role.

It's important to focus on the main backbone of your codependent role(s). The controller may feel "less than" like a dependent but rises to power and controls the dependent. The controller does not stay in a "less than" default setting and does not need to be rescued or saved. The controller is the rescuer and false god. The dependent may at times feel he is rescuing someone in a relationship but will usually rescue by dishonestly "people pleasing." The dependent needs to be emotionally rescued and has a deep, inherited "less than" and shame based default setting. The dependent role also will experience the embedded and programmed "failure fix."

360 Degrees Of Codependence
Write a "D" for Dependent and "C" for Controller, below.

Example:
35 year old clean and sober male addict.
Rotation pattern: Male addict has a dominant controller role, with a secondary dependent role.

Grandparents – C with my dependent grandmother
Parents and/or stepparents –
C with my dependent mother
D with my controller father.
Brothers – C with my dependent younger brother.
Sisters – N/A (not applicable).
Past and present intimate relationships – C in all my romantic relationships. My second girlfriend out of high school, I was a D but relationship ended after a few months.
Work related and business partners – D toward my present day controller boss.

Write C or D next to your relationships below. Two addicts in a relationship will sometimes rotate, but one of the roles is usually dominant. You can write CD if you rotated during a relationship with another addict and your controller role was dominant. Or write DC if you rotate during the relationship and your dependent role was dominant.

Example: *Female addict has a dominant dependent role, with a secondary controller role DC.*

My first husband is an addict with a dominant C and secondary D. I rotated during the relationship and was mostly a DC.

My second husband is a controller (not an addict) and I was a D with no rotation to my C.
My third husband is an addict with a dominant D and secondary C. I rotated during the relationship and was mostly a CD.

From the example above, the female addict rotated with another addict but had no rotation with a one split controller. Remember, two addicts in a relationship will rotate their two codependent roles but one is usually dominant.

Place your C, D or DC, CD next to the family member, relatives, friends, work relationships, intimate relationships, etc.

Grandparents –
Parents, stepparents and role models –
Brothers –
Sisters –
Aunts –
Uncles –
Godparents –
Cousins –
Past and present intimate relationships –
Your children –
Friends –
12-Step sponsor –
Sponsees –
Work related – business partners, manager, etc -

For the one split codependent: Controller or Dependent

If you are a *controller,* you will see several C's listed throughout your surrounding relationships with dependents. These relationships create the addict's loop between you and the dependents in your life. If you are a dependent you will see several D'" listed throughout your surrounding relationships with controllers. These also create the addict's loop between you and the controllers in your life. Both codependent roles may have relationships with codependents with the same role. Controllers may have lots of controller friends and dependents may have lots of dependent friends. These relationships do not create the addict's loop between them because they tend to agree with each other and neutralize the addict's loop.

For the addict

When you review your 360 degrees of codependence, the inner circle will be your family and all romantic relationships/partners and significant role models. The outer circle will be friends and employment relationships, etc. Add up your C's and D's and identify your rotation pattern. Do you evenly rotate, or is one of the codependent roles dominant, with a secondary back seat role?

Which description below fits your rotation pattern?

Evenly Rotates – Addict will attract, gravitate and evenly rotate from the *controller* and *dependent* in all her relationships. For example, an addict in an intimate relationship with a *controller* breaks up, in the next relationship is a *dependent*, breaks up, and then gravitates back to being a *controller*. You don't have to rotate exactly 50/50, but experience close to an even pattern.

Dependent Role Is Dominant – The addict's dominant personality is the *dependent* role, with the *controller* role in a secondary, back seat position. Addict will mostly attract and gravitate to another addict who has a dominant *controller* role with a back seat *dependent* (CD) or a one split *controller* (C).

Controller Role Is Dominant – The addict's dominant personality is the unconscious *controller* role, with the *dependent* role in a secondary and back seat position. Addict will mostly attract and gravitate to another addict who has a dominant *dependent* role with a back seat controller (DC) or a one split *dependent* (D).

Step 6
Uncover your original unconscious pain load and inherited behavior in the two codependent roles.

The one split codependent should answer the questions directed toward his one codependent role.

Your codependent role(s) have traveled many generations and ended up in your unconscious. It was never about you being a bad person, unlovable, flawed or broken. It was never about you not being good looking enough or smart enough and never adding up. It has always been about the *original unconscious pain load* that has destroyed millions of codependents and addicts with the same inherited programming and behavior. The goal is to become aware of the multi-generational inherited behavior and separate yourself from it. Generations of codependents and addicts have experienced the same embedded and destructive unconscious programming. Each behavior will vary with its *"charge."* You might be affected by all the inherited behaviors, or only a few.

Below is what I believe to be the original unconscious behavior embedded in the two codependent roles of the *controller* and *dependent*.

The Dependent's Inherited and Programmed Behavior

I get angry and withdraw when the controller doesn't fix my broken life. My default setting is defective and flawed, and I unconsciously return to this default setting to be rescued and saved by my controller. I'm disconnected from my true feelings. Most of the time I cannot identify how I feel, and dishonestly "people please" to feel accepted and loved by my controller. I will repeat my broken behavior and set myself up (failure fix) to be routinely criticized, lectured and judged by my controller and then resent, reject and abandon him. I fear my controller's anger. My controller must take care of me, but I rarely feel satisfied and always want more. I do not feel in control of my life and need my controller to direct me. I stay with my controller and allow him/her to criticize, lecture, judge and abuse me to avoid my fears of rejection and abandonment.

Give an example of how the dependent's programming and behavior relates to your own life.

1) I get angry and withdraw when the controller doesn't fix my broken life and take care of me. *Give an example.*

_____

_____

_____

_____

_____

_____

2) My default setting is defective and flawed, and I unconsciously return to this default setting to be rescued and saved by my controller. *Give an example.*

_____

_____

_____

_____

_____

_____

_____

_____

_____

_____

3) I'm disconnected from my true feelings. Most of the time I cannot identify how I feel and dishonestly "people please" to feel accepted and loved by my controller. *Give an example.*

_____

_____

_____

_____

_____

_____

_____

4) I will repeat my needy and broken behavior and set myself up (failure fix) to be routinely criticized, lectured and judged by my controller, and then resent, reject and abandon him. *Give an example.*

_____

_____

_____

_____

_____

_____

_____

5) I fear my controller's anger. *Give an example.*

_____

_____

_____

_____

_____

_____

_____

_____

6) My controller must take care of me, but I rarely feel satisfied and always want more. *Give an example.*

_____

_____

_____

_____

_____

_____

_____

7) I do not feel in control of my life and need my controller to direct me. *Give an example.*

_____

_____

_____

_____

_____

_____

_____

_____

_____

_____

8) I stay with my controller and allow him/her to criticize, lecture, judge and abuse me to avoid my fears of rejection and abandonment. *Give an example.*

_____

_____

_____

_____

_____

_____

_____

_____

The Controller's Inherited and Programmed Messages

I fear my dependent cannot function and will possibly die if I do not rescue him from his/her broken behavior and life. I will rescue and enable my dependent so he/she feels connected and loved and I feel in control and valued. I'm critical, demanding and judgmental, and sooner or later I will be rejected and abandoned by my dependent. I give too much, keep track of my generosity and then resent my dependent and become a victim of his/her self-centered and broken behavior. I will never feel satisfied and will always need more love, praise and attention from my dependent. I will solve my dependent's life problems and will always feel superior and resent his/her weaknesses and flaws. I will never allow my dependent to become equal or more powerful, fearing my dependent will abandon me.

Give an example of how the controller's programming and behavior relates to your own life.

1) I fear my dependent cannot function and will possibly die if I do not rescue him/her from his broken behavior and life. *Give an example.*

_____

_____

_____

_____

_____

_____

_____

_____

2) I will rescue and enable my dependent so he/she feels connected and loved and I feel in control and valued. *Give an example.*

_____

_____

_____

_____

_____

_____

_____

_____

_____

_____

3) I'm critical, demanding and judgmental, and sooner or later I will be rejected and abandoned by my dependent. *Give an example.*

_____

_____

_____

_____

_____

_____

_____

_____

_____

4) I give too much, keep track of my generosity and then resent my dependent and become a victim of his/her self-centered and broken behavior. *Give an example.*

_____

_____

_____

_____

_____

_____

_____

_____

5) I will never feel satisfied and will always need more love, praise and attention from my dependent(s). *Give an example.*

_____

_____

_____

_____

_____

_____

_____

6) I will solve my dependent's life problems and will always feel superior and resent his/her weakness and flaws. *Give an example.*

_____

_____

_____

_____

_____

_____

_____

_____

7) I will never allow my dependent to become equal or more powerful, fearing my dependent will abandon me. *Give an example of how you might make the dependent feel "less than," so you can feel powerful and needed.*

_____

_____

_____

_____

_____

_____

_____

_____

_____

_____

Step 7
Identify your personal unconscious pain load which continues to recreate itself.

The one split codependent should answer the questions directed toward his one codependent role.

The goal of this step is to create awareness and separation from your unconscious pain load, which you have created with your codependent family and role models during your child/teen conditioning years.

The Dependent Role

The codependent and addict's dependent role *echo shames* and believes they deserve the pain load passed down to them. The dependent role will then recreate the handed-down abuse and become a target in his surrounding codependent relationships. The dependent role usually passes his pain load *passive aggressively.*

Example: a male addict who has a dominant dependent role and secondary back seat controller role. During his child/teen years, the dependent child was told by his controller father that he was stupid and would never amount to anything. The controller father might rarely have said this, but his expressions, sighs, glances and other behavior *charged* the negative message to his son's dependent role. Remember, the dependent role already has the self defeating multi-generational message, so it does not take much conditioning for the dependent to echo shame and self-contaminate his core identity. Once the negative message has been conditioned and learned, the adult addict or codependent will gravitate to similar abusive relationships and re-create the abuse and be a victim that continually re-experiences the message of *"never being good enough."*

Another example: a dependent who was beaten by his controller parent. Because the parent is a controller to the dependent role, the addict or codependent will think he somehow deserves the abuse and will repress and protect it. Later in life, the addict or codependent can gravitate and recreate his abuse with another controller who also abuses him. The abuse is enmeshed with the euphoric high/fix on the addict's loop and creates the unconscious damaging behavior and message *"To feel loved and connected, I must also be abused."*

The Controller Role

The controller role can be a victim of another controller's abuse and the dependent's repressed rage. The controller usually does not believe he deserves his abuse and pain load. The controller will usually be aggressive and pass his abuse and pain load directly to the dependent.

Review your 360 degrees of codependence and make a list of

the controllers and dependents you rotated during child/teen years.

1) In your dependent role, who were your controllers and what emotional pain and abuse have you received, believed you deserved, protected and made excuses for in your family and significant role models during child/teen years?

Below is an example of an addict's codependent inventory. Several pages were written, but for the purpose of example, the text has been shortened and edited.

Example: *Female Addict– Clean and sober six months. Addict is a dominant dependent role with secondary back seat controller role.*

Answer to question 1. *My family controllers are my alcoholic father (rotator with dominant controller role and secondary dependent role), my uncle (controller role) and my older sister (controller role).*

Father - *I have always loved and feared my alcoholic father. My father loved us, ruled the house and would stand in front of a truck to save his kids. A few times, when he was drunk, my father sexually abused me. I have protected my father's abuse and kept it our secret for most of my life. Two years ago, when I was in treatment, I finally told my counselor. I have always believed I did something wrong and it was my fault that I was sexually abused. I have also made hundreds of excuses and looked the other way for my father's drunken behavior. (shortened and edited)*

Uncle - *I have always felt judged and never good enough around my uncle. I know my uncle loves me, but he makes me feel insignificant and stupid. Whenever I talk to my uncle about my hurt feelings, he usually turns it around and makes me feel that I'm the over-sensitive and crazy one, and I end up feeling like a bug on his windshield. I know I allow my uncle to make me feel like a piece of crap, but for some reason I keep needing his approval. (shortened and edited)*

Sister - *My sister is my best friend and pretty much runs my life when I'm using. We love each other, but if I don't follow her directions, she gets very angry and becomes a total bitch. I get overly sensitive and entitled around her and borrow money, which I rarely pay back. My sister gets very angry at me but has always protected me and controlled my crazy life. (shortened and edited).*

Use note pages at end of book for extended writing.

_____

_____

_____

_____

_____

_____

_____

_____

_____

_____

_____

_____

_____

_____

2) Looking at your dependent role, what abuse and pain have you recreated and repeated in your adult relationships with controllers outside of your family?

Continuing example: Addict - *clean and sober six months.*

Answer to question 2. *I feel I'm being haunted by my father's abuse and uncle's condescending view of me and seek it in other men. It's sickening. I try to prove that I'm worthy, but deep down inside I feel undeserving. My recreated abuse from childhood has allowed my intimate relationship controllers to emotionally hurt and abuse me, like my father did. I feel like I'm wearing a target on my back when I enter into a relationship with a controller. Most of the time, I believe I somehow deserve the abuse, or they manipulate and convince me it was my fault (just like my father). Also, I have allowed my intimate relationship controllers to take advantage of me sexually. I feel like a sexual object and fear they'll leave if I don't do what they want. I'm always walking on eggshells and end up depressed and hating them. When I leave the relationship, they beg me to stay and promise they'll change. For some crazy reason, I think my love can change them but it only seems to make it worse. (shortened and edited)*

My dependent role with my uncle and my recreated abuse is somehow finding controllers that always make me feel like a bug and a total idiot. The manager at my last job was extremely controlling, condescending and abusive. He would constantly make condescending remarks whenever I screwed up. I usually acted like it didn't hurt and showed no emotions but later when I was alone, I would get very angry, cry and get depressed. I was afraid if I said anything wrong and didn't kiss his butt, he would fire me. He also made several inappropriate sexual remarks and advances. I ended up hating him and quitting my job. When I'm in my dependent role, it's extremely difficult for me to set boundaries and protect myself against powerful controllers. (shortened and edited)

I also tend to surround myself with controller friends that baby me and tell me what to do. It makes me feel taken care of, but I can tell they're disappointed when I relapse or don't follow their directions. They usually abandon me, or I feel shameful and cut them off. I feel like my dependent role is a ghost in my head,

119

always telling me I'm a piece of crap and can't do anything
without the help of a controller. (shortened and edited)

3) In your controller role, who have you rescued, enabled and abused in your family and significant role models during child/teen years?

Continuing example: Addict - *clean and sober six months.*

Answer to question 3. *My family dependents are my mother, my father's sister (Aunt Kay) and my brother, who is a dependent and possible addict-rotator ... the jury is still out.*

Mother- *As long as I can remember, I have protected my mother from my father's drunken anger and abuse. My mother treats me more like a sister than a daughter and has always shared her personal problems with me. I pity and resent her for not being able to stand up to my father, and I also resent her for being selfish and not being a good mother to me, my older sister and brother. I feel if I don't control her life and help her, she'll fall into a miserable depression and never come out. (shortened and edited)*

Aunt- *I love my aunt, but she is a bottomless pit and rarely goes outside or visits my family. My aunt is a hypochondriac and the most neurotic person I've ever known (besides myself). My aunt has permanently nailed herself to the cross and whines about her life, and then becomes deaf, dumb and blind when I give her solutions. I love her, but she's totally frustrating to talk to and be around for any length of time. One thing for sure, the dependents in my family, me included, are experts at baiting the controllers to rescue them. (shortened and edited)*

My brother- *I believe my younger brother is also an addict. I know he is a dominant dependent, possibly with a secondary controller role (just like me). I love my little brother and worry about him all the time. My father was very hard on him, and nothing my brother did was ever good enough. My little bro is a pot head, and I try not to do any drugs around him, but we usually end up getting high and laughing about our screwed up family. (shortened and edited)*

_____

_____

_____

_____

_____

_____

_____

_____

_____

_____

_____

_____

_____

4) Looking at your controller role, what childhood abuse and pain have you recreated in your adult relationships with dependents outside of your family?

Continuing example: Addict- *clean and sober six months.*

Answer to question 4. *I have been in two intimate relationships with dependents and had several friendships which I've cut off, or they just faded away. The first intimate relationship was with an addict who was a dominant dependent with a secondary controller role. The relationship lasted around eight months and was extremely passionate and draining. The relationship quickly became about me rescuing his lazy ass. I thought he was cool and funny in the beginning of our relationship. He moved into my apartment, got fired from his job and expected me to buy all his drugs, and then he refused to move out when I asked him to leave. We spent most of the relationship fighting and arguing. I do remember punching and slapping him a few times. His entitlement issues suffocated me, and we ended and started the relationship several times over an eight-month period. I finally had to get a restraining order because he wouldn't leave me alone. Last I heard, he was in jail for possession. As I'm writing this, I really see the addict's loop. I was attracted and blinded by his cool, and it got me high, which then became a nightmare, and the relationship fell apart by the loop's betrayal, rejection, abandonment into a hell hole. It's really true that I get totally blinded by the dependent's cool and can't see the hell waiting around the corner. (shortened and edited)*

_____

_____

_____

_____

_____

_____

_____

_____

_____

_____

_____

_____

_____

_____

_____

_____

_____

5) Reviewing your codependent role(s) what patterns, are you now aware of in your surrounding relationships?

Continuing example: Addict- *clean and sober six months.*

Answer to question 5. *I'm now aware that I have not emotionally left my family, and continue to play out my inherited codependent roles in most of my relationships. I'm either a draining, dependent vampire or a controlling maniac. I've also noticed that I can rotate both roles in a relationship with another addict. One hour I can be a dependent, the next hour a controller. The weird thing is, I was completely unaware I was rotating between both codependent roles and recreating the abuse and hurt feelings I experienced growing up with my family.*

My sister has always told me that I'm looking for my daddy in a relationship, but I now believe I'm looking for the same codependent experience I had with my dad. I've been living and rotating both these annoying and horrible codependent roles all my life, and I know it's not going to change overnight, but I would like to graduate from my family's incestuous codependent insanity and stop recycling the same abusive crap. (shortened and edited)

_____

_____

_____

_____

_____

_____

_____

_____

_____

_____

_____

_____

_____

_____

_____

Step 8
Reclaim your core identity and learn to live in your proactive present.

Proactive Present: A proactive "here and now."

The one split codependent should focus on his one codependent role.

Step 8 begins to counter condition your codependent role(s) and reclaims your echo shamed and abandoned core identity. *This shift out of the unconscious controller and dependent role(s) and into your core identity is the shift out of addiction and codependent patterns.* During this shift, you will be challenged by the "tug of war" between your reclaimed core identity and unconscious codependent role(s). Your codependent role(s) and your childhood conditioning have created years of unconscious programming and behavior that will take time and patience to counter condition. With your new awareness, small adjustments can create powerful and positive shifts out of unconscious codependence and the addict's loop.

Your Echo Shamed Core Identity

You have returned home to your echo shamed and abandoned core identity. Imagine your emotional life as a swimming pool that your inner child was told to pollute and abandon. Returning to your echo shamed and contaminated swimming pool, you will probably experience a feeling of relief, anger, frustration, fear, anxiety, "highs," "pink clouds" and "lows." The waters can get very rough, but they will stabilize over time as you continue to counter condition your internal codependent role(s). It will take courage and forgiveness to reclaim your core identity and learn to navigate from your new spiritual center of gravity.

With your new awareness and knowledge, you, the now clean and sober adult, take the hand of your inner, traumatized child, and together you reclaim your abandoned core identity with a new sense of belonging and renewal. The goal is transitioning from addiction "fixes" to "cultivating" your life from your proactive present. Cultivation involves footwork and allows the seeded footwork to grow at its own pace and time. Cultivation involves a measured degree of controlled footwork, and then letting go of the results.

Your Proactive Present

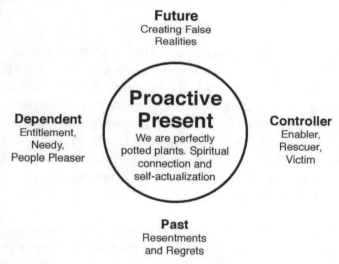

Living in your Proactive Present

Future
Creating False
Realities

Proactive Present
We are perfectly
potted plants. Spiritual
connection and
self-actualization

Dependent
Entitlement,
Needy,
People Pleaser

Controller
Enabler,
Rescuer,
Victim

Past
Resentments
and Regrets

Visualize a circle around yourself. It may help to use a large hula hoop or draw a chalk circle. Inside the circle is your "proactive present." This is where you self-actualize without interference from the unconscious codependent role(s). Inside the circle, you learn to cultivate and plant seeds of footwork for your goals, solutions and life. On two 3" x 5" cards, write "controller" on one and "dependent" on the other. Place one card to your left and the other to your right, outside the circle. On two similar cards, write "future" and "past." Place the "future" card outside the circle in front of you and the "past" card outside the circle, behind you. If you are a one split codependent, use one card that represents your codependent role. The goal is to stay in the center of your circle, your spiritual center of gravity, your proactive present.

The codependent role(s) and addict's loop will unconsciously gravitate the addict and codependent out of their proactive present. The addict and codependent have been conditioned to gravitate into their future of false fears and doom, or into the past and beat themselves up, become victims, and resent the people that hurt them. The addict and codependent gravitate out of their proactive present and become the entitled and broken dependent, and/or they rotate and gravitate outside the circle and become the rescuing and enabling controller.

All gravitation points are outside the addict's spiritual center of gravity and seek a "euphoric high/fix." Basically, whenever the addict or codependent is outside the proactive present they seek a "fix" to escape their fears and return to a sense of connection, security and wholeness. Unfortunately, we have learned to do this through the destructive codependent role(s). The addict and codependent's euphoric high/fix creates a *temporary illusion* of being connected and whole and then every time reveals its destructive lie and betrayal.

It is important to be patient when counter-conditioning your unconscious codependent role(s). The addict's and codependent's unconscious knee jerk reaction is to immediately gravitate outside their circle into the *land of the fix*. The addict and codependent seem to magically transport themselves and awaken in the codependent role(s) and their victimized past and bleak future. Counter-conditioning becomes an awareness game. I will usually "awaken," or become aware, when I'm outside my proactive present, and then make adjustments to return back to my proactive present. This takes practice and is a process. It is important to be extremely patient with yourself and this process. You can think of it as learning a new language or musical instrument.

For most of my life I existed in the *land of the fix* and believed that was my core identity and deep truth. It's easy to get stuck outside your proactive present circle. That's where most of us have lived our entire life. The long-term goal is to gradually catch yourself before you step outside your proactive present. The new counter conditioned awareness and behavior becomes, *"I feel drawn to this controller and must be aware not to lean and be needy and abandon myself into my dependent role,"* or *"I'm attracted to this person who shows all the signs of being a needy, entitled dependent. I must be aware and not rescue and enable him."* This powerful awareness becomes your new default setting and keeps you inside your proactive present circle.

Below are some examples of the codependent and addict gravitating outside his proactive present.

Example: You've made a commitment to help your sister move into her new apartment. She is depending on you to help pack and load her rented moving truck. You receive a phone call from your manager at work, who is a controller and has triggered your dependent role. Your manager wants you to work on your day off and hints that there will be layoffs next month and that it'll look good if you show up and work today. You immediately become fearful and visualize yourself unemployed. You begin "people pleasing," and tell your manager you'll be there in an hour. *You have gravitated outside your proactive present into your dependent role, and have created a fearful and false future of unemployment.* In the proactive present diagram, you would step outside the circle onto your dependent card, and then walk to the future card in front of you. This mechanical is a visualization for when you are fearful, confused and in emotional pain. By closing your eyes and visualizing your circle, you can ask yourself a few questions: *"Where am I outside my proactive present? What codependent role did I gravitate into? Did I gravitate into a bleak and doomed false future or my resentful past?"*

Example: Your romantic "dependent" partner gets fired from his job and needs to borrow money from you. You lecture him about finding employment, tell him where to look for a job, and criticize him about his disastrous employment history. You end the conversation by telling him that he'll never change. *You have gravitated into your controller role and into the resentful past and* *false future.*

Example: You're in your proactive present doing footwork and trying to find a better job. You send out six resumes, make three networking phone calls and place your resume online. You finish, and become depressed. You think "what's the point, things will never get better." *You gravitated into your dependent role and false future.*

These are a few examples. The goal is to become aware of gravitation "hot spots" that trigger and transport you outside your proactive present. As you become aware of your gravitation, you'll discover what "hot spots" outside your proactive present you consistently end on. Example: *You might be a controller that gravitates and consistently ends on your resentful and victimized past or an addict whose dependent role consistently ends up on the future, creating a scary, false future.*

Over a period of time of practicing and becoming aware of your gravitation outside your proactive present, answer the question below.

Do you consistently gravitate outside your proactive present in a codependent role, into your past or future? Write where you find yourself consistently gravitating.

_____

_____

_____

_____

_____

_____

_____

When you identify a consistent pattern, it's important to uncover the pain beneath your gravitation.

Example: You discover you consistently gravitate in your controller role to your resentful and victimized past. *This could mean you attempted to rescue a dependent that continually abandoned you during child/teen years.*

Example: You discover you consistently gravitate in your dependent role into a false future filled with fear and doom. *This could mean you were raised by a powerful controller, that you desperately attempted to "people please." Your controller would rescue you and then harshly criticize you and make you feel "less than." Your unconscious fear and message became,"My life will always betray me and become bad thing."*

Example: An addict with a dominant dependent role and back seat controller. The addict discovers he gravitates in his dependent role to his resentful past and beats himself up. The addict's internal messages are, "Look at the mess I've made, I always screw things up, I cant do anything right." *When the addict inventories his gravitation, he discovers that during his childhood he was blamed for most of the bad things that happened with his controller mother. The codependent child "people pleased" to feel connected and repressed his painful feelings on the right side of the addict's loop.*

What pain have you discovered from a codependent relationship that makes you consistently gravitate to the same place outside your proactive present?

_____

_____

_____

_____

_____

_____

_____

_____

_____

_____

Remember, when you gravitate outside your proactive present, it doesn't mean you've failed. This is a process of catching yourself, uncovering and discovering your gravitation pain, processing it, making necessary changes and adjustments and setting boundaries back into your proactive present.

Step 9
Counter-condition the addict's loop by living in your proactive present and nurturing abundance without addiction fixes.

The one split codependent should focus on his one codependent role.

We do not belong in our codependent role(s)' fearful and doomed future, or resentful and victimized past. We belong in our proactive present. In our proactive present we do not control and enable another person's emotional life, or lean on him until he/she breaks. In our proactive present we become truly connected, aware, balanced and responsible.

Counter-Conditioning The Controller Role

In the addict's loop, the controller's programming rescues and enables the dependent and then becomes rejected and abandoned. Dismantling the addict's loop means staying out of the false connection and its negative programmed behavior. To achieve this, there must be a new awareness of where the controller's power is useful and where it destroys. Standing in your proactive present, the controller learns to make suggestions without expectations or manipulating the results. The controller releases the need to enable, rescue and save the dependent. The controller realizes this is a false and destructive definition of love and is programmed, every time, to betray, reject and abandon. The dependent might unconsciously manipulate and demand to be saved. The dependent may even abandon the controller for not rescuing and enabling him. *The controller must risk everything to be free.*

When the dependent wants the controller to fix a life problem, the controller can say, *"I believe in you and know you'll figure out your problem."* Instead of the controller saying, *"You're doing the wrong thing and making the wrong choices,"* the controller can say, *"If you want, I can make some suggestions."* If the dependent is open for suggestions, the controller can suggest "A, B or C" and then allow his partner, friend or family member the freedom to choose one or none of them.

One of the biggest shifts for the controller is to give up his power and control over the dependent to feel loved, praised and valued. The controller now realizes this is not love, but a path of destruction. The controller stands in his proactive present and accepts himself, without controlling and manipulating the dependent. The new question becomes, *"Who will love and respect me if I'm not powerful and controlling?"* Standing in your proactive present is accepting and loving all of yourself, your talents, flaws, your brokenness and great abilities. Standing in your proactive present, the controller surrenders being a destructive false god over the dependent. When the codependent or addict stands in his proactive present, fears of abandonment may become overwhelming and create anxiety. Remember, this is the insidious lie and con of unconscious codependence and over time the anxiety can pass. In our proactive present, we learn to be truly connected with our root honesty and our spirituality and learn to love without hurting ourselves and others.

Counter Conditioning The Dependent Role

In the addict's loop, the dependent is programmed to be broken, needy and entitled. Standing in your proactive present, the dependent learns to be responsible and begins to risk and make his own choices and decisions. The dependent learns that he is allowed to make mistakes, learn from them and grow. The programmed dependent role wants the codependent and addict to believe she will always be "less than" and fail. The dependent's multi-generational programming sends the unconscious broken message, *"I cannot survive alone, and the controller must rescue and take care of me."* Counter-conditioning these unconscious messages will take courage and patience. The dependent lets go of neediness and entitlement, with a new understanding that the dependent role's inherited programming creates a destructive and false connection to feel secure and loved. Becoming aware, and counter-conditioning the dependent role's programmed behavior, allows the dependent to become connected, self-reliant, responsible and whole.

The Shift Out Of The Two Codependent Roles, Into The Proactive Present.

The one split codependent should focus on his one codependent role.

We negotiate, share and manage chores in our relationships. We control and fix cars, lawnmowers, microwaves, sewing machines and plumbing, but we do not fix and control other people and do not expect other people to rescue and enable us. We control and manage our work, but we do not control and manage our partner, friends, and our family's emotional and spiritual life. When you continue to exercise healthy boundaries in your proactive present, you will begin to experience a new freedom, joy and happiness. Below is an example of the dependent and controller's destructive and false connection in the addict's loop and new counter-conditioning behavior.

A dependent is waiting for a controller who has promised to get him a job at his company. The dependent feels entitled, doesn't look for employment, and waits for the controller to fulfill his promise. The controller wants to be the dependent's hero and be praised, but is unable to get the job for the dependent. The controller never wants to be seen as a failure, so the controller keeps the dependent baited and hopeful. Over time, the dependent begins to resent the controller for not getting him a job, and the controller resents the dependent for leaning on him. They end up blaming and abandoning each other.

In the example above, the dependent and controller are standing outside their proactive present in the *land of the fix*. The dependent wants the controller to "fix" his unemployment, and the controller wants to "fix" the dependent and be the hero, feel praised and valued. The controller learns to end his control, enabling and manipulation. The dependent's shift and counter-conditioning into the proactive present would be to stop leaning on and feeling entitled toward the controller. The dependent stands in his proactive present and asks himself, *"What can I do in my proactive present to solve my unemployment?"* The dependent's footwork becomes the seeds that are planted inside his proactive present circle. The dependent's measured control and footwork might be networking, calling friends about employment opportunities, cold calls, updating and sending out resumes, searching job forums on the internet, etc. The seeds the dependent plants in his proactive present may begin to sprout, or not. If they do not sprout, more controlled footwork is needed. If a job opportunity develops from the footwork, this becomes a path the dependent learns to nurture rather than sabotage. *Remember, controlled footwork is conscious footwork that also creates healthy, conscious negotiations in relationships. Codependence is <u>unconscious control</u> (no awareness) that destroys.*

It is important to be aware that the dependent role is programmed to sabotage its proactive present and self-actualization process. The dependent can reject doing footwork because he/she unconsciously wants the controller to "fix" his life. The dependent's actions of finding employment can cause anger, resentment and feelings of abandonment to surface. These unconscious feelings can make the dependent appear lazy and indifferent. The reality is, the multi-generational dependent role has been programmed to sabotage itself and not be able to move forward without the controller taking charge and running the show. The deep unconscious programming stops the dependent role from being proactive and responsible. Over time and practice, the dependent's proactive footwork can counter-condition the destructive unconscious programming and behavior.

My proactive present diagram can also be used as a meditation circle. Sitting with your eyes closed, you can visualize yourself in the center of the proactive present circle. Here, in your *spiritual center of gravity,* you are free of unconscious codependence. In your proactive present, you do not lean and feel entitled, or over-control and enable anyone. You are not in your future creating scary stories and not in your past beating yourself up and being a victim. Inside your proactive present is where you learn to love with measured boundaries. With continued proactive awareness and action, the codependent and addict builds a new and healthy self-esteem and self-respect. It is in the proactive present that we truly self-actualize our emotional life, talents and abilities and learn to nurture them into abundance without sabotaging our efforts.

My nine-step process for counter-conditioning addiction and codependence should be revisited and become an ongoing process for your path toward self actualization and freedom from the unconscious codependent role(s).

Chapter 11

From The Introduction Of Book.
Answering My Questions About Addiction

What creates addiction?

The addict inherits both codependent roles, the controller and dependent, which are permanently separated in the addict's unconscious. Both roles idle and create the dependent's embedded and programmed "less than" feelings and the controller's loss of control and powerlessness. These become the main two psychological triggers that motivate the addict's internal rescue mission. The two unconscious roles cannot connect and rescue each other unless there is a catalyst. The catalyst is the addict's euphoric "fix" (alcohol, drugs, sex, gambling, etc.) that temporarily merges and fulfills the addict's internal "rescue mission," between his two internal codependent roles. During the addict's substance use, the dependent is transformed and feels connected, rescued and safe and the controller feels powerful, bigger than life and in control. At the peak of the internal rescue mission is the euphoric high/fix on the addict's loop. The addict's internal rescue mission and "high" is only a "temporary fix." When the addict's drug of choice ends, both codependent roles reawaken and discover they're disconnected, abandoned, separated and alone in the addict's unconscious. This awareness triggers the addict to seek the euphoric high/fix on the addict's loop and once again recreate his internal "rescue mission" between his two codependent roles.

Why do some people become addicts and others don't?

To become an addict you must have both codependent roles, the *controller* and *dependent*, conditioned in your unconscious and also inherit the *biochemical loop*. It is my belief most *rotators* will inherit the biochemical loop. These two loops feed each other and create a self-drowning affect. If a person has one codependent *split* (either a controller or dependent) and gravitates to the opposite codependent role, she can create substance and behavioral *abuse* or the *illusion of addiction* during a codependent relationship.

Why do some addicts become full-blown in their teen years and others later in life?

The beginning of addiction depends on the conditioning and *charging* of the two codependent roles. If a child's home is *highly charged* and the child has inherited the two codependent roles and has a predisposition to the addict's biochemical loop, the child/teen may progress into full-blown addiction in his early teens. If the addict's codependent roles are not *charged* enough and the addict is still navigating from his core identity and root honesty, addiction may start later in life when the addict gravitates into a codependent relationship that triggers the addict's loop.

Why are addicts in denial about their addiction?

Addicts are in denial because they have been conditioned to block out the right side of the addict's loop and biochemical loop *(betrayal, rejection, longing, abandonment, non-existence, plus withdrawal, detox, craving, abandonment and depression)*. Addicts are obsessed with the left "attraction side" *(longing, connection, love bond, euphoric high/fix, plus, craving, preparation, connection, euphoric high/fix)*. Because of this dynamic of being blinded by the euphoric high/fix and blocking and repressing the denial side of both loops, addicts experience their addiction as a powerful blind spot and continually make excuses for their destructive behavior and substance use. Simply, they cannot see the *rejection, abandonment and hangover* waiting around the corner because it has been completely blocked out on both loops.

Why do some addicts come from loving homes where no addiction, abuse or trauma occurred?

The codependent family can be loving, caring and nurturing, but codependence is still covert and passed in the family system. The dependent child will perform and "people-please" and be seen as the child/teen everyone loves and gets along with. The controller can be seen as the "can-do kid" and high achiever. Parents and society will validate these roles and the child/teen will continue *charging* his false and dishonest performances and protect his destructive roles and accept them as the norm. Even though the child/teen was deeply loved and never abused, his codependent family system and two rotating codependent roles can create enough disconnectedness, powerlessness and shame to trigger the addict into his *internal rescue mission* and create addiction.

What can families do to help an addict they love?

Begin to counter-condition their own codependent role(s). Once they learn to set boundaries and stay out of their codependent role(s), they will begin to help themselves and the addict they love. If they do not counter condition their codependent role(s), the families' unconscious codependence will continue to fuel the addict's two codependent roles.

What causes the Dr. Jekyll and Mr. Hyde personalities of addiction?

During the addict's euphoric high/fix, the repressed anger from the right side of the addict's loop can surface and create a "Dr Jekyll and Mr. Hyde" effect. The likable, "people pleasing" dependent *rotates* and becomes the angry and loud controller addict. The controller will usually take a back seat position and the likable dependent is the dominant personality in the addict's life. The addict's substance and euphoric high/fix creates a venting pathway that surfaces the back seat controller. The back seat controller might only surface during intimate relationships and be covert in the addict's life. Most of the addict's friends may be shocked to see the loud, raging, controlling personality surface, but someone who has shared an intimate relationship with the addict might comment, *"Oh yeah, I've seen that side before."*

Why does addiction progress and lead to insanity and sometimes death?

As the unconscious pain load is recreated, it progressively builds, infiltrates and finally flatlines the addict's euphoric high/fix on the addict's loop. As the unconscious pain load surfaces, the unconscious "waves of pain" continually need to be numbed with substance use. Even though the euphoric high/fix has been trumped, the addict's loop continues to send a message to recreate its self-rescue mission with it's two internal codependent roles and substance. As the two loops progress the two codependent roles or the dominant role will become amplified. The unconscious programming will continue until the addict "awakens" from the two loops, bottoms out or progresses into insanity and death.

Does an addict love his addiction more than his loved ones?

The addict wants more than anything to love his family, intimate relationships, friends, etc. That is the great tragedy with unconscious codependence and addiction. It is because the codependent and addict child did not feel loved and accepted that he abandoned his core identity to survive and feel secure and loved. As the addict recovers and learns to uncover and counter-condition his codependent roles, he can slowly begin to rebuild his life and learn to love from his core identity and build healthy, loving relationships.

What is the cure or strongest treatment for recovery?

Unfortunately, I believe there is no cure for addiction … yet. Once the codependent roles have been inherited and conditioned, they are set for life. The addict must learn to manage his two codependent roles and stay out of their programmed behavior. I strongly believe it is our responsibility to create awareness, education, workshops and intensive counseling to counter-condition codependence in the addict's unconscious. Many addicts leaving treatment have never heard the word "codependence" or "codependency" and do not understand its deeper networking and programming. I have met many codependents and addicts who have read every book on codependence and still do not know the difference between the *controller* and *dependent* roles. As long as the addict's hard-wired codependence and relationship *charging system* is intact, the addict will unconsciously be pushed toward relapse. Clients entering treatment should begin counter-conditioning their codependent roles immediately after detox. Through the process of treatment, addicts must learn to recognize and set boundaries to stay out of their two codependent roles. This treatment should continue and be monitored and counter-conditioned for several months after the addict transitions from treatment to sober living or next step in life.

In closing.

Unconscious codependence and its programmed behavior makes us believe we are broken, unlovable, disconnected and alone. It is the cruelest and most destructive lie that continues to be passed onto our innocent children and future generations. We must awaken and counter-condition codependence from its deepest roots; otherwise, its brilliant con will continue to pass its shame, denial and destruction. When a population's *original unconscious pain load* becomes more powerful than its *conscious awareness*, it is doomed to a path of self-destruction. My hope is that *The Addict's Loop* will become a starter kit to begin the process of uncovering and counter-conditioning codependence at its deepest roots. If we do not awaken and counter-condition codependence patterns, our children will continue to be programmed for addiction, destructive relationships, disorders, illnesses and spiritual emptiness. It is our present-day challenge to reawaken our true spiritual connection and begin to reclaim our authenticity.

Chapter 12

Glossary

I have placed an asterisk* next to my own definitions, unique to my addiction and codependence model.

*Addict's Loop – An unconscious, revolving door pattern that creates a euphoric high/fix and then blocks and represses any rejection, pain and abuse. The loop is created from the attraction of the *dependent* and *controller* roles. Ascending pattern: *Longing - Connection - Love Bond - Euphoric High/Fix.* Descending pattern: *Betrayal - Rejection - Longing - Abandonment - Nonexistence*

Authentic Self - Refers to the self-actualized and genuine person; who you really are at the collective core of your being.

*Biochemical Loop - Conditioned biological loop: *Craving - Preparation - Connection - Euphoric High/Fix - Withdrawal - Detox - Craving - Abandonment - Depression.* I believe the biochemical loop was created from the addict's loop. Both addict's loop and biochemical loop work together to completely destroy the addict.

*Charging System – The addict's surrounding relationships create a *charging system* that fuels the addict's loop.

Codependence - Defined as a psychological condition or a relationship in which a person is unconsciously controlled or manipulated by another who is affected with a pathological condition (addiction or illness). In broader terms, it refers to the unconscious dependence on the needs of or control of another.

Controller - Also know as "false god" or "hero controller." The unconscious codependent role is inherited and learned during child/teen years. The child learns to dominate, enable, rescue and save the dependent role.

Conscious Pain Load - The codependent and addict's conscious awareness of abuse, emptiness, hopelessness, shame, guilt, remorse, despair, sadness, etc. These feelings and experiences are accessible and can be expressed and shared.

Core Identity - The central, innermost, or most essential part of ourselves. This also can be your authentic self.

Dependent - The unconscious codependent role is inherited and leaned during child/teen years. The dependent child is programmed to be broken, shameful, needy and feels entitled to be rescued by the controller.

*Echo Shaming - The unconscious conditioning of a dependent or controller receiving critical and shaming abuse and making it his/her own pain, inner voice and central experience. The child unconsciously abandons himself and performs the maladaptive codependent role(s). I believe this process is how codependence is passed down through the generations.

*Euphoric high/fix - An obsessive, self-centered blind spot codependents and addicts gravitate toward and desperately attempt to control and manipulate to feel powerful, connected, whole, loved and secure. The euphoric high/fix creates the illusion of being rescued and elevated above the codependent or addict's conscious and unconscious pain load.

*Fixing Charge - The unconscious motivation to reach the euphoric high/fix on the addict's loop. The *fixing charge* is motivated by the conscious and unconscious pain load. For example, the more powerful the addict's fears of rejection and abandonment, the more powerful *fixing charge* to reach the euphoric high/fix is needed in order to escape the surfacing pain load.

*Gravitation - The codependent and addict's unconscious attraction to their destructive roles and behavior.

*Land Of The Fix - An unconscious world, outside our spiritual center of gravity, where the addict's loop continues its revolving door pattern of the euphoric high/fix and then *betrayal, rejection, abandonment and fear of nonexistence.*

Man-Made Hell - Man's fiction and non fiction lies, fears, torture, ghost stories, rituals, superstitions, barbaric practices, abuse, rage, emotional pain, shame, guilt and/or depression are repressed and stored in the unconscious or denial side of the addict's loop. The collective repressed chaos of these emotions and experiences creates and conjures our mythological monsters and demons recreated in ourselves, our relationships and our exterior world.

*Original Unconscious Pain Load - The inherited controller and dependent roles, their destructive programming, embedded messages and unconscious pain load passed through generations.

*Unconscious Pain Load - The codependent and addict's <u>repressed and</u> <u>unidentifiable</u> fears, emotional pain, shame, guilt, rage, abuse and trauma stored in the unconscious or reservoir of denial in the addict's loop. For example: a dependent gets fired from his job. His *conscious pain load* might be fear, insecurity and anxiety mixed with false projected fears of financial ruin. The *unconscious pain load* is the dependent's betrayal, rejection and abandonment from his controller business partner who triggers and surfaces old childhood pain from the addict's loop and reservoir of denial.

*Pain Load Peak - When the unconscious pain load surfaces into consciousness.

*Proactive Present - Navigating life proactively from our core identity and spiritual center of gravity in the proactive "here and now."

*Root Honesty - Our deep instinctive honesty that is interfered with and destroyed by the codependent role(s).

*Rotators - An addict who has both *controller* and *dependent* roles conditioned and permanently fixed in his/her unconscious. The addict rotates between the two roles, which ultimately leads to his or her destruction. Both roles can be rotated equally, or one of the roles can be dominant while the other takes a back seat position.

*Spiritual Center Of Gravity - The perfect conditions to self-actualize and fulfill our wholeness and genetic blueprint. The spiritual center of gravity for a plant is the balanced amount of soil, nutrients, sun, water, etc. The plant's spiritual center of gravity would have no interference to hinder its growth and development.

Subconscious - Exists below consciousness. For example, subconscious can be where you store your street address; you may not be thinking of it right now, but if asked, you could pull it up from your subconscious.

*360 Degrees Of Codependence - Unconscious gravitating and *charging system* with relationships that surround the codependent and addict.

Unconscious - Below our conscious and subconscious radar, completely unknown to us.

Notes:

Notes:

Notes:

CPSIA information can be obtained
at www.ICGtesting.com
Printed in the USA
FSHW010503170820
73030FS

9 781496 049476